GROUND GLASS

GROUNDGLASS

KATHRYN SAVAGE

COFFEE HOUSE PRESS
Minneapolis
2022

Coffee House Press books are available to the trade through our primary distributor, Consortium Book Sales & Distribution, cbsd.com or (800) 283-3572. For personal orders, catalogs, or other information, write to info@coffeehousepress.org.

Coffee House Press is a nonprofit literary publishing house. Support from private foundations, corporate giving programs, government programs, and generous individuals helps make the publication of our books possible. We gratefully acknowledge their support in detail in the back of this book.

LIBRARY OF CONGRESS CATALOGING-IN-PUBLICATION DATA

Names: Savage, Kathryn, 1985– author.
Title: Groundglass / Kathryn Savage.
Description: Minneapolis : Coffee House Press, 2022.
Identifiers: LCCN 2022008400 (print) | LCCN 2022008401 (ebook) |
    ISBN 9781566896405 (paperback) | ISBN 9781566896481 (epub)
Subjects: LCGFT: Essays.
Classification: LCC PS3619.A833 G76 2022 (print) |
    LCC PS3619.A833 (ebook) | DDC 814/.6—dc23/eng/20220304
LC record available at https://lccn.loc.gov/2022008400
LC ebook record available at https://lccn.loc.gov/2022008401

PRINTED IN THE UNITED STATES OF AMERICA

29 28 27 26 25 24 23 22   1 2 3 4 5 6 7 8

For Dad and Henry.

For the daughters of a place and the mothers.

When I say *fathers* I imagine the picture of my gentle father with his brother (dead now) and his mother (also dead) and his father (now also dead, although at the time of first writing *not* yet dead), laughing, no one looking at the camera and no one noticing the photographer, who must be a friend or maybe my uncle on my mother's side, and who is in the room but invisible, and who for us has handed down these bodies as they once were, and outside the room the crush of history goes on

—Éireann Lorsung, *The Century*

Error, disease, snow, sudden weather.
For those given to contemplation: this house, . . .
viewing on groundglass an inverted image.

—Muriel Rukeyser, *The Book of the Dead*

GROUND GLASS

Humboldt Industrial Area

Trains at night, keening. Years ago, in Victory, a street dead-ended into a large railroad switching yard, bright-lit, voices of men carrying. I can remember the noise of industry coming through the screened windows of my childhood. The place I'm from has long been a magnet for illegal dumping.

Once, a warehouse fire at the Howe Chemical Company, located in the industrial area, burned over one hundred different pesticides. Water to put out the fire washed pesticides and fertilizer into Shingle Creek, named after the asphalt-shingles manufacturing plant nearby. Soils and groundwater were polluted from runoff, so berms were built to pond the water on Howe property, to keep runoff from traveling farther into the backyards, our rhubarb stalks and tomatoes. The watershed. Eventually, the Mississippi River.

One day in high school, I come home to my father taking a sledgehammer to the back walls of our house. Wood floor matte with sheetrock dust. He wants a wall of glass, has a sliding door he's pulled off some jobsite to brighten the view. A hole in our house opens onto the backyard, where he's stacked lumber, PVC pipe, sheet metal, and cinder blocks. Before he illegally installed the solar panels that heat our home, they'd been used to warm a catfish farm. He keeps propane tanks in the grass; they cap with snow in winter. The spring before, his project was a garage addition. He rented a backhoe to dig the trench. Before the frost came, he dug forty-two inches below the frost line; poured the concrete footing, on top of which he lay block; backfilled the trench; and then added the anchor bolts, the sill plate, framed the plywood subfloor.

"Learn how to build this," he always told me, and I tried to keep up. A room was composed of layers. It had depth and hidden parts. Together we made rooms. That day, so many years ago, he walked me over to his newest project: he'd framed one eight-foot wall and needed me to hold the beams. I lifted them; they were heavy.

He's dead, and I replay this memory.

Curtains

"Join the club," my friend said over drinks, handing me the book *Some Thing Black* weeks after I stood in the crematorium where a man I did not know and would never see again pushed a button and I watched my father's body move toward flame in a cardboard box with our surname scrawled in marker on its side.

On that day, I had been bothered by and too aware of the curtains over the window that separated me from him. Chintzy pink satin, heavy pleats. The man who worked the button asked if I wanted to see. I realized the question was if I wanted to see my father's body burned to ash. I said I did. The curtains parted slowly, loudly. I stood. I looked. I said, *Stop.* I understood why they were there.

Or it was like this: In the *Republic,* Socrates tells the story of a man, Leontion, who came upon dead bodies lying on the ground at the place of execution. He felt a desire to see them, and also a dread and disgust; he struggled and covered his eyes, but at length the desire got the better of him, and pulling his hand from his eyes, he ran up to the dead.

My father's body was on the other side of glass. I felt a responsibility to look. I was his only daughter. Looking can be many things, and one of those is love.

The book *Some Thing Black* was strange. This made me love the friend who'd given it to me more, because my grieving was strange.

Jacques Roubaud wrote *Some Thing Black* in the years after the sudden death of his wife. It is a transcription of his loss and the ever-present "not-there-ness" of her—her things, his memories. Roubaud writes: "Through simple repetition of *there is no more* the whole unravels into its loathsome fabric: reality."

While my father was in the hospital, his diagnosis and the particularities of his disease were presented on during a medical conference. I was standing in the hallway outside his ICU room, talking to his surgeon, who had done the presentation. The conference attendees had been very interested in my father's gastric cancer and its unusual progression, he said, as if paying my father a compliment. I knew by then that his cancer occurs at a slightly higher rate in areas that produce industrial waste and pollution. Was what made it unusual that we had long lived on the fence lines of industry? Was it the outside toxins within his body? It would be impossible to know, the surgeon said. What was and was not possible tethered us to the questions his body posed.

He died because his body was unwell. The industry we'd long lived near was a part of his cancer, I was coming to see, or maybe this was paranoid. It crossed my mind that it could be both, but I didn't yet know how.

I couldn't watch his body burn, but I decided I could visit the Superfunds.

The Soo Line Dump

Drought pales the dip of meadow coming into view. Treed and ryegrass-covered, this place is unrecognizable as a former rail dump. Today, the dog pulls hard at the sight of a coyote up ahead. I've seen rabbits and pheasants here other days; watched birds building nests. The low hills of the dump are between the off-leash run and the fence with No Trespassing signs. Across the fence is Shoreham Yards, the 230-acre polluted train, trucking, and bulk-distribution site two blocks from my house.

Up ahead, a structure of wood. At first I think it might be where someone is living, but closer, it is a discarded shipping pallet with a rail tie over the bed. Maybe I keep coming here because as much as this is a site of burial, it is imperfect. No ruin but active. Diesel particulates catch the breeze. Nothing from the past peeks through the tallgrass, but I know that the surface and subterranean, past and present, meet here.

It is June; ephemerals line the fence. Snow trillium and skunk cabbage. Across the chain-link, the U.S. Department of Health and Human Services Agency for Toxic Substances and Disease Registry has determined this brownfield to be vast and complex with significant petroleum and solvent-related soil contamination reaching deep below, down to the water table, and impacting groundwater.

The dump poses questions of scale, perception, and concern. What has died here? What grows from the violent soil?

Walking, I think about Terry Tempest Williams visiting the Great Salt Lake to grieve for her dying mother and also the wounded water basin. "Death is no longer what I imagined it to be," she writes. It is not a vacancy but a crowding and "earthy like birth." She cannot prove or disprove that her mother developed cancer after being exposed to atomic bomb tests in their desert home in the 1950s, but one night, she joins nine other women who trespass together, entering "the contaminated country." "The women couldn't bear it any longer," she writes in her memoir of personal and ecological grief.

Were the women restless, tired of waiting? It seemed some days that he was both dying and not dying. How to be with what is happening invisibly and relentlessly? The women walked onto a testing site to protest the long abuses of the land. When they were arrested, after being questioned about why they'd come, they answered back: "We are mothers and we have come to reclaim the desert for our children."

Shoreham Yards, Minneapolis, Minnesota. Aerial image of Shoreham Yards and the neighborhood that surrounds the industrial site.

Live Map

At night, while my son is upstairs in his room, I scroll the EPA's Superfund National Priorities List live map. Topography strung with confetti flecks. Each colorful fleck aligns with one of 1,322 national priority sites, which are severely polluted places.

There are another 450,000 active brownfields, old polluted industrial sites, across the country, like the rail dump I walk past to the dog park, but no interactive map for such sites. They are common places to find lingering environmental contamination dusting dandelion leaves or the screened windows of living rooms.

The volume of polluted places overwhelms. A dailyness sinks in. The map sprawls. I scroll images of demolished mills and smelters. Pit mines. Long veins of creeks and rivers. Fields where grasses bend, exposing young pale shoots. Upstairs, Henry laughs, playing video games.

On Openings

When my son was breastfeeding, I was always leaking. My shirts smelled like hot milk, slightly sour.

Months before, I'd gone to the ultrasound alone the day I learned my bloodstream wasn't providing adequate nutrients and oxygen to my baby. Something to do with the placenta, it had started to "shut down." I asked the doctor what to do but there was nothing. I ate sugar so my child would squirm. Dig a bony elbow into me.

Years later, I will learn that if a woman cannot consume sufficient calcium, her body will take from her bones to give to her infant. That toxins can be passed in breast milk. Body burden—the load of environmental pollutants bodies hold—can be transmitted genetically, so it is intergenerational, becoming a strange inheritance.

The placenta is the environment shared by mother and fetus. Particulate air pollution the mother breathes can harm placental health, so a question I will ask myself, later, is: what place-history coursed in my blood? When I heard the words "placental insufficiency" I was twenty-four and had worn calf-high boots to the appointment. It was September. In the obstetrician's curtained room, the child's body lit on-screen. Later that night, my child's father, who loved me, was terrified for us, but I felt good, young and strong, walking briskly up the stairs to our apartment.

When my body became an emergency, my child came out early. The placenta was tested by a pathologist in a lab. The test results were inconclusive; clotted pit pulled out of my low abdomen, then chucked. I never held the wild pomegranate but if I rounded with life again I'd make them give it to me. A smear off someone's blue-gloved hand. Arsenic, tetrachloroethylene? I'd conduct my own examination.

Returning

I go back home. This isn't such a dramatic return, only a four-mile drive along roads that hug the Mississippi River. June. The sky blue as a pool. My son's at his elementary school and I've got the day off work, so I drive past the industrial corridor north of the Lowry Avenue Bridge. A metallic sharpness rides the breeze. Here are the same industries that have dominated these riverbanks for more than a century. The tar-shingles factory, power station, concrete producer, two plywood and lumber suppliers, and an acrylic fabricator.

I park on the cul-de-sac before the maroon-trimmed house. The small white house that held my small white self and small white dog, beside track carrying oil bound for other cities. Oil that leaked onto earth. Two decades later, the pine tree in the front yard is plump and bushy, gorgeously tall.

Some days, kids play by the high fence spooling vines that divide this street from the rail yard. I did this with my friends two decades ago, kicking a soccer ball in the flat, open patch of grass.

I started coming back after his funeral.

When he stopped working the odd construction job, as his disease advanced and his memory declined, his bills were mailed to my house. Some days, there would be cleanup reports from Canadian Pacific Railway in the mail about Shoreham Yards, the polluted rail yard at the end of my block that connects, by miles of track and history, to the polluted yard I grew up near, Humboldt Industrial Area. The yards crisscrossing the Mississippi.

In 1872 Horace W. S. Cleveland advocated for a Minneapolis city park system that preserved open space for public use but left this stretch of river out. The waters south of Saint Anthony Falls—two miles downriver and closer to downtown—would have parks and trails along the banks, but city planners, wealthy landowners, and businessmen deemed this northern water too valuable as a place of commerce.

People who live along this stretch of river in North Minneapolis suffer from the highest rate of asthma-related hospitalizations and the highest concentration of lead poisoning cases in the state. North Minneapolis remains one of the hearts of the Black community in Minnesota. It was a place where people experienced poverty and oppression in Minneapolis. This stretch of river is a layered ecology, where 140 years of industrial use, expansion, and plant, animal, and human life coexist. "No patient is sovereign," Anne Boyer reflects in *The Undying,* the memoir she wrote after her cancer diagnosis. We are all "marked by our historical particulars, constellated in a set of social and economic relations."

This stretch of river is my home. How common is a lifelong proximity to industrial contamination sites? Who else held similar stories in their bodies? According to the findings of a 2020 EPA report using census data, approximately 200 million people live within three miles of a Superfund remedial site or brownfield, which is roughly 61 percent of the U.S. population. The racial and income inequities among impacted populations are stark. Of the 21 million people who live within one mile of a Superfund, 49.8 percent of the residents are described as minority and low-income populations in the most recent EPA site census demographics report available at the time of this writing. Terri Hansen, reporting for *Indian Country Today* in 2014, writes that 25 percent of all U.S. Superfunds are located within the boundaries of sovereign tribal nations, on tribal lands. All U.S. land is Indigenous land; this legacy of violence and trauma to Indigenous peoples predates the fund.

In a moment of dialogue between Anne Boyer and her daughter, in Boyer's memoir, she comforts her daughter with the good results of a genetic test: her daughter's genes do not predispose her to cancer. "You forget," her daughter replies, "that I still have the curse of living in the world that made you sick."

We were poor, our lives an inconvenience to our neighbors, capital. It was nothing revolutionary I was confronting through my father's death, just the hard truth that disease can be accelerated by lived experiences. By our proximity to extractive capitalism and legacy pollution, a structural inequity that unjustly impacts, locally and globally, communities of color and Indigenous peoples and low-income people of all races and ethnicities the most. Fence-line communities are also called "sacrifice zones."

I hold this place, this maroon-trimmed house, this block of complexity and inequity, in my body in the form of memory, and in the form of industrial particulates that inhabit me epidemiologically, and in the form of grief.

Walking my old neighborhood, I stopped to sit beside Shingle Creek. It had rained heavily the night before. The water was high up the sandy banks, propelling what floated along: today, a hunk of driftwood, splayed candy wrappers, a plastic Coke bottle. This one artery flowed urgently toward a point of confluence. I watched the water move.

Teaching Hospital

One night, when I am seventeen, breathing hurts and doesn't stop. My lung has collapsed. I am treated at a teaching hospital. A tub wedged between my ribs. Medical students move in and out of my room. Classes come to study me. What had happened inside me was unusual in such a young woman, the doctors say.

At the teaching hospital, no one asks if while my lungs were developing I lived near an asphalt-shingles plant, a city refuse, a sooty switching yard. I am not suggesting that the air pollution I was exposed to as a child caused my body to breach. But to the curious, because I had moved away from my old neighborhood by then, the presumption of geographic permanence that necessitates such comparisons is limiting. I believe such limits of the imagination foreclosed the asking of the questions.

Put differently, Rebecca Altman, an environmental sociologist who studies body burden, the load of pollutants bodies hold, reflects, "To study body burden is to learn how to read the historical archive stored in flesh and blood and bone."

Day Drives

In the elementary school parking lot, I close my eyes until my son unlatches the door. Dinner before the television again. I fix a drink. Fix a hard smile on my face. Say too often and brightly, "Everything's good."

Then I'm parked near a pile of tar shingles. Pink, plastic-wrapped bundles stacked like bricks. Sparrows swoop. The tight ropes of muscle in my neck go slack. My body is like hard cheesecloth most days, stiff, saturated, but tears come at the sites. My father is dying; or, he has been dead a day, a week, a month.

After adjunct teaching, contract work for low pay, I go to the sites. After donating my father's eyes to science, after donating his car to Goodwill and then waiting in a long line at the Social Security Administration to complete the death forms, I go to the sites. Saying, "He's dead," in tall buildings or on the phone. Unpacking the proof and handing it across the table. My eyes catch on the certificate: *Place of Birth: Winnebago. Manner: Natural. This is a true and correct record of death.*

Keisha Brown

"Keisha Brown was 12 the first time she stopped breathing," I read online. Keisha grew up in Birmingham near a Superfund, falling asleep to trains moving past her bedroom window, "where carloads of coal traveled from the industrial site across the street through the quiet backyards of her neighborhood." One night, she woke unable to breathe.

There is a picture of Keisha's house that I look at for a long time. Her white house with turquoise trim reminds me of the house where I grew up. It is across the street from "moss-covered hills" that "are really mounds of industrial waste." A fence encircles more than four hundred acres of waste mounds on land that was once a dairy farm. There's a No Trespassing sign with the warning: "Potentially dangerous conditions may exist in this area."

Keisha has long suspected her own asthma was a result of living in a polluted neighborhood. It crosses my mind that though we are strangers, maybe we've lived similar experiences from a geographical and ecological perspective.

I write to her because it's like my friend Kate says, "I don't like how we're never going to know the answers, but I like knowing it together."

She writes back the next day. "Call me."

Harriman Park, Birmingham, Alabama. Aerial image of the neighborhood that surrounds the Thirty-Fifth Avenue. North Birmingham Superfund site.

From: Keisha Brown

Thirty-Fifth Ave. North Birmingham Superfund Site, Alabama

At night, lately, I can't sleep. Can't sleep because the trains vibrate my house. I grew up here. I've been here all my life. I want to leave because the air it seems worse now. We need to be evacuated.

This is what I want to know: Why are we overlooked so much? Is it because we're a Black community? All of us who are living here are Black. EPA people are still out here digging, still digging, still digging. Still putting dirt here and dirt there. Dirt is not helping us.

The problem is inside my body, not in my yard.

Before, a lot of people would have miscarriages. Now they're saying these chemicals that people got in their bodies—benzene, naphthalene, arsenic, lead, and benzo(a)pyrene—affected them carrying a baby. That's why they had the miscarriages. A lot of them have female problems still, you know?

It was summer, June of '89. We had to evacuate, but we still don't know what chemicals we were exposed to that day. We should have been told but they just told us to leave. This was my first time ever seeing the fire department and they had hazmat suits on. There on my front porch was a fireman who looked like an astronaut. He scared me. We had no warning.

My grandma came into my room and said we had to leave immediately. I got my mom. She was taking a nap. She had worked the overnight shift at the nursing home the night before. We had to get out of the house, and when we came back hours later they said it was O.K., but we watched the news, all of these firemen, it was a hot summer. June is hot. They had hazmat suits. What did we have?

Nobody was tested. We don't know who did what undercover, but we were never tested for what we were exposed to in 1989.

They brought city buses in. We went over to my aunt's house across town and stayed until about five or six, and then we went back home. Somebody should have set up some medical thing to check our blood, our breathing, but nothing was checked, nothing.

Some people had four or five miscarriages and they didn't know why.

I will miss living in this house. It is beautiful. It's home. My grandfather had this house built by a Black construction company in 1950. He moved here from South Alabama and got a job working at a steel pipe plant. He worked there for years.

In the mornings, on his pillow, he'd see residue from the dust he'd inhaled working at the plant.

Outside, today, soot from the trains leaves ugly marks on the siding and window trim. Lots of local businesses have moved out. We used to have more stores here, a gas station. Drive-through restaurants. It was a nice middle-class neighborhood.

Over the years, they put this big pile of coal-distilling byproducts across the street from my house. People think it's a mountain. If you pull it up on Google Earth, you will think, "Oh, you got a mountain across the street from your house." But no, it's not. It's a mountain of chemicals. It's a coke-making byproduct that they use to pave the street. It's called raw material. It's been there over twenty-something years, just sitting there. When the wind blows, it gets into your nostrils.

Right next to that is the railroad track, the cement plant, and the coal plant. The train moves coal, which is not covered. It's just terrible. It's like they used our neighborhood as a dumping site. We're like the city dump out here.

They say this is a site of cleanup, but you can't clean up what's constantly coming down. I don't understand that logic. They give us all these stipulations, saying, "Be careful. Don't let your kids play outdoors." You can't stop kids from playing outdoors!

They say: "If kids go outdoors, make sure they take a bath." Well, you bathe your kids when they come in the house, anyway. "Wipe your feet off. Don't drink or eat in your yard. Don't chew gum." You know, people have get-togethers. We should have the right and privilege to eat, drink a soda or a bottle of water outside. Sit in our yards, relaxing.

But it's got to be all these stipulations, like I'm in prison in my own home. People need to be moved out of here, moved from this situation.

We should have been evacuated already. I'm thinking about down in New Orleans. The UN rapporteur on contemporary racism called the continued industrial projects along the Mississippi River in St. James Parish—they call it Cancer Alley down there—a serious and dispro-portionate threat to human rights, to the right to health, and the right to an adequate standard of living. Many of those same chemi-cals are here too. St. James Parish is a Black community and so are we.

We can't grow a garden. They told us that about ten years ago. Can't grow a garden because it's so contaminated, so we can't grow food.

If we can't grow a garden to have the basic necessities, vegetables and food for our families, we have to buy food at the store, which is a high price, and we have a food desert here.

It's all a form of imprisonment. It's always *no, no, no, no*. When does a *yes* come? When is the positive stuff coming in?

At a forum with government agencies, they had the Alabama Department of Environmental Management, ASTDR, EPA, and all the different people from CERCLA—everybody was there. I told them, "We have too many limitations to live in this place. You tell us we can't do this, can't do that. It's so bad we want to leave." I had my own yard checked for contaminants some years ago. They tested it. Told me I had eleven out of fifteen chemicals. I say, one chemical is bad enough.

I work with a local group, the Greater-Birmingham Alliance to Stop Pollution, or GASP, and we have been doing a lot. When the pandemic first started, it was hard to get toilet paper, hand sanitizer, even food out here. We stepped in and started bringing people cooking oil, flour. I called my neighbors to see what they needed. We offered people meals.

Then last May, we started a pop-up. A pop-up market where people can get free fruits and vegetables and eggs and household stuff. Really, it's a grocery. A free outdoor grocery store.

Now that pop-up is in three neighborhoods. We're feeding over one hundred or two hundred people or more, because people are coming from other neighborhoods. Even other counties up here. We do a lot. We get our fruits and vegetables from this farm, they donate it, and it's so fresh. We give so much that each person ends up with two or three bags of groceries apiece.

It's hard. I pray about so many things. I take a lot of vitamins. People take medicine out here. One person might take enough pills for two people to function. Ninety-five percent of the community is sick with something.

Asthma and cancer, skin disorders, all kinds of strange stuff. It was so strange—all these kids with asthma. They said we had the highest level. It was terrible.

The companies keep saying they're in compliance, but the fact is that people are getting sick, and those chemicals are going in people's yards and bodies, we're inhaling it, and the trains are always shaking, vibrating our houses.

I feel, personally, that instead of the millions of dollars they have spent in these communities the last ten to twelve years remediating, they could put a subdivision in an area that's not contaminated, that's near no industry, and build new housing for this community as a whole. They're wasting money just digging. They're even digging on empty lots where nobody lives. The people are dead, the whole family dead, so really, they're not helping the situation. It's a disservice. Some places are unlivable.

My birthday is on Mother's Day, but I'm going to celebrate on Saturday, with a honk-and-blow. People will drive by and honk their horns, bring gifts. My son is twenty. So you know how it is. Some days, I feel like an amoeba or a paramecium; it feels like I did it all by myself or something. But hey, that's life, and it's good.

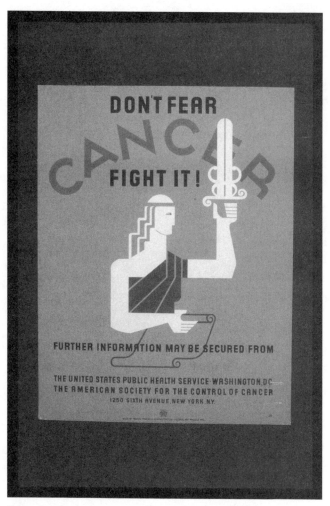

Poster promoting treatment for cancer, sponsored by the Federal Theatre Project (New York City, New York) between 1936–1938.

Exposure

Dancer Isadora Duncan died when her enormous hand-painted silk scarf tangled with the rear hubcaps of her sports car in Nice, France. I'm reading S. Lochlann Jain, queer studies scholar and medical anthropologist. Death in many forms, Jain reminds, including hand-painted silk scarves.

A defining feature of cancer is the vague root cause. Smoking? Genetics? Plastics? Where is cancer? Jain asks, "Is it in the body or in the culture around it?"

I've come to Jain's work to probe the neoliberal "cancer survivor" trope. I distrust the survivor trope, as does Jain, who writes about the blurry line between environmental exposures and disease in their work *Malignant: How Cancer Becomes Us*. There are no burning shingles or volatile organic compounds in the language of cancer or its survivors. One is diagnosed as individual. If many, only that of kin. Genetics and personal habits alone enter the arena of cancer's battle.

My father wanted to survive. After each treatment he spoke about working hard to be well again. The hospital's medical pamphlets emphasized good nutrition, sleep.

The survival rate for my father after diagnosis was less than 6 percent. Nonetheless, all the year he was dying, he was overworked but intoxicated by his own working.

I am not against hope, certainly not opposed to the effort to stay alive in the face of disease, just wary of how central individualism is to cancer's mythology. The cancer patient is a sole embattled cellular warrior rarely aligned with the social or environmental.

At the hospital, we never discussed pollution with his oncologist. So when I write about it I feel specious, like someone who suspects their spouse of an affair. All is my own hushed theorizing, *and yet*—

To accept individuality as at the heart of cancer fails to map culpabilities between extractive industry, illness, and displacements. As Jain writes, "Framing survivorship as a personal accomplishment further separates cancer causation from its manifestations."

Narrative anxiety is inseparable from late capitalism and its violence that obscures connections. Through obscuring, in the case of cancer survivorship—premised on an individual battle to be won or lost—it implicitly absolves industries that perpetuate exposures to carcinogens from legally compensable responsibility for causing such injuries. More devastatingly, it scrubs those industries clean from cancer's imaginary.

It is an act of violence for a system to ask an individual to surmount by resolve what cannot individually be surmounted.

I feel close to Jain when they write: "In searching first for the everywhere- and nowhereness of environmental exposures," the point to linger on isn't the if/then. Maybe if the environment is cleaned up cancer will go away, but no one knows yet, so maybe not. What are "the broader costs of accepting the general lack of proof, despite serious suspicion, about cancer's causes."

What are the costs for imploring a dying person to fight for a life they can never have?

Façade has allures. I've long lived near tar-shingle factories and polluted waterways, above toxic groundwater, and beside crude-oil transport pushing along on outdated lead track. I've accepted a general lack of proof of the dangers because such acceptance gives me a feel of control over my body and what enters it. A general lack of proof as physical safety is an affectation and a false equivalence.

It wound around the axle, Duncan's scarf, and tightened on her neck, and dragged her from her car. "Affectations," said Gertrude Stein when she heard the news of Duncan's death by scarf and sports car, "can be dangerous."

View of a neighborhood home from the Humboldt Yard industrial site.

Toxic Sites

"Standing before you, I ingest you. There is nothing fanciful about this. I am ingesting your exhaled air, your sloughed skin, and the skin of the tables, chairs, and carpet in this room."

—*Mel Y. Chen, "Toxic Animacies, Inanimate Affections"*

I sit on my couch watching TV with my boy, reading about bulk chemical and petroleum storage two blocks away; today's soil and groundwater cleanup, tomorrow's too.

Here, mailboxes hold quarterly cleanup-progress newsletters— data about nearby hazardous waste circulating in air, soil, and water beneath.

Statistics of great volume fill the mailers. How the chemical heft of twelve grand pianos has been hauled away over the length of a decade—6,000 pounds of volatile organic compounds, emitted gases from solids and liquids; 6,409 pounds of pentachlorophenol— pumped from the groundwater.

A hole in a well was recently found leaking and repaired on-site. Structures boast a longer life expectancy. I am thinking of deep layers of my father's stomach wall rupturing, how his body kept opening, rejecting management. I think about the notion of a gut feeling, all the trust metaphors a stomach holds. How affective the land underneath me is, with its wellholes leaking like a wrecked human body.

Mullein

I live in a 1909 Sears two-story with patinaed wood floors that turn the shade of expensive honey in morning light. I bought this house after I divorced because it was close to my job and my son's school. Built on a limestone foundation over deep wells of vinyl chloride–contaminated groundwater, a heavy robin's-egg-blue wedge atop sandy soil. After moving in, I planted a rain garden. My front yard a tangle of milkweed, woodland strawberry, great blue lobelia, rose turtlehead, honeysuckle, Jacob's ladder, prairie smoke, and wild golden glow, denser every year.

"The mullein is back," Gudrun says. We are drinking wine on her front porch, her dog splayed and running in sleep between our two laps. My friend and neighbor, who has noticed more of it this past summer, hairy biennial whose stalks are skirted with a large rosette of sage-green leaves, lining her backyard fence line. She says mullein grows crooked when the soil is chemically contaminated. At the end of her block is a playground where we took our sons when they were small, sharing soil with Shoreham Yards, ringed by mullein, tilting shadows in the dusk.

Safe

From the *East Side Shoreham Newsletter*, I learn the name Louise. Louise works for Canadian Pacific. I call, leave a vague message, and am surprised when she calls me back. We talk for a while, I ask my questions. I tell her I want to see it. "What *it?*" "The roundhouse," I say. "It was demolished earlier this summer," she tells me. "Even if it was still standing, you couldn't see it. This is an active worksite." I am nodding my head in agreement, though Louise cannot see this. I know about active worksites; I want Louise to know I know. "We don't just let people onto the rail yards. You can't come in here unless you have business," Louise says. Do I have business? Business isn't mothering or my dead father. I breathe the rail yard; I eat it in the tomatoes I grow out back. I tell her quite impotently that I receive the *East Side Shoreham Newsletter*. I am a regular reader of it. That I didn't know about any of this until I moved into the neighborhood, just two blocks away from the roundhouse. I tell Louise my address. Her voice shifts. A wall is erected. She says, "People know about the pollution here, the public has been informed." I concur. I do feel more informed, daily. She tells me there used to be community meetings on the cleanup status, but attendance dwindled so the company stopped hosting them. Then she tells me I am safe. My tap water is safe. My yard is safe. They have been remediating volatile organic compounds since the 1980s. I am so safe. I like the way Louise says the word. She sounds authoritative and maternal. I want to keep her on the phone. I want her to keep telling me.

A Series of Symptoms

Yesterday, driving to teach, I watched a man sample a well. His testing equipment, thin coils, spiraled down the vapor hole. The pollution at Shoreham and the soil vapor extraction are the reasons padlocked metal pipes that look like lean hacked tree trunks line the neighbors' boulevards. From these rusting pipes into the air, volatile organic compounds, which sound thick as heavy cream but are gases, are intermittently released from the soil and the groundwater.

In her essay "Is All Writing Environmental Writing?" Camille T. Dungy writes about ecotones, "areas at the margins between one zone and another—like the tidal zone where beach and ocean overlap, or the treed and grassy band where forest becomes meadow—spaces that are often robustly productive and alive." I live in a polluted ecotone, a porous patch of neighborhood where two systems that shouldn't merge have, and one violates the other. Dungy seeks to "de-pristine" her environmental imagination, and so do I. She asks writers working now, "in the midst of the planet's sixth great extinction," witnessing, participating in, or being subjected to "the direct effects of radical global climate change," to consider how we're describing the natural world and ourselves in it in our work.

Earlier this year, a railcar roundhouse built in 1887 was demolished at Shoreham to make way for a paved lot to house empty shipping containers. If one pillar of the capitalist violence of gentrification is erasure, then the building left a trace of the long, complicated histories—extractive, industrial, racial, social, economic—that persist here. Its presence echoed. The building, unsafe as it was, visibly animated unseen dangers. It was a ruin of witness.

My house faintly shakes from the paved-lot construction. There's a creosote odor in the air. Two weeks ago, there was a pipeline break at the site. One of the above-ground conveyance pipelines was damaged when it was struck by heavy equipment. The pipe was moving contaminated groundwater to a nearby treatment facility. Seventy gallons of impacted wastewater were released. The break happened during a heavy rainstorm.

Shoreham is a voluntary investigation and cleanup, a VIC site. At VICs, mandated cleanup of industrial toxins takes place while land use goes on. The name makes them sound gentle and considerate, like a well-behaved child who makes their bed in the mornings without needing to be asked.

Brownfields and VICs are environmentally degraded, but to what degree? Unlike Superfunds, such neighbors as these can have less public stigma attached to them. Here the roads are repaved in spring. Good public schools and parks are a short walk away. There's a co-op down the block, in a large eco-friendly building.

I like living here. Maybe I am as complicit as the rail yard. I desire this place for my use too. I have been asking myself, *What would true remediation look like here, ecologically and culturally?* A restoring, a redress. It would be reparations; the end of settler violence; land back; my absence.

On and off throughout this neighborhood's extractive industrial history, manufacturing and distribution yards have been bought and sold; risks to human health posed by onsite pollutants have crossed thresholds, some have subsequently been remediated; and what of today, I wonder, the newly broken pipeline moving contaminated groundwater off-site; the unearthed soil, smoky sky?

A week later and the air still smells like creosote. Fall. Leaves sharp and bright under slate clouds. There's a familiar thudding at the end of the road, trucks backing up, engines rumbling on. The paving of the storage slab is well underway.

Construction crews are also installing a stormwater pond. Stormwater will make its way the mile to the Mississippi River. The pond can be seen through a fence that divides the yard from a cemetery. Spied from the cemetery, the pond looks deep—deeper than CP Rail told the surrounding community it would be at a recent public meeting. The impermeable liner promised for the pond has not been installed yet. Looking through the fence one day, the pond is gray green and ordinary. Two ducks glide across the surface.

I am concerned that toxic dust from the soil they're digging up under the demolished roundhouse is blowing into surrounding yards, coming in open screened windows. It's been a windy fall. Are the dirt piles supposed to be tarped, covered? Has the soil been recently tested? When the wind isn't blowing, it's raining, flooding the stormwater pond. Two of us go back to the cemetery and take pictures of the water. One of us contacts an environmental specialist from the state pollution control agency. We learn that the soil and debris at the yard have been tested and the majority of samples don't exceed MPCA's residential soil reference values. The contaminated soil will be hauled to a landfill, we are told, to fill the belly of other land.

Site contaminants haunt. What I believe is that our lives may be affected by the rail yard's contaminants in ways that would be difficult to prove in epidemiological studies. Maybe one day it will be found out that I am like the roundhouse, a site of toxicity, a form holding a place-history in my folds. Maybe I'll be hard to decontaminate. Meanwhile, wind blows loose dust wherever it does and an unanswered series of questions stir in me. I breathe and eat and go on living, same as any other day.

In her book *Critical Ecofeminism,* Greta Gaard includes epigraphs and journal notes as marginalia beside her more scholarly writing. The effect lends an embodied phenomenological approach to topics that range from milk to fireworks to animals in space. In one entry, Gaard writes, "In the month that I begin to write about climate change, my body begins to sweat. I wake in the night, flooded with heat. The warmth begins at the base of my skull, then curls up my head and around my neck like smoke curling under a closed door. The heat pours down my neck and shoulders, arms, spine, leaving me sweating, then chilled. Nothing is wrong. This sudden heat is a step toward my own mortality, natural and inevitable. I think about what it is like to be a body, overheating."

I've felt what Gaard describes. It was during the year I stopped breastfeeding my son. That year, I developed a series of symptoms. It could have been no more than a recalibration of hormones after I stopped feeling the deep thirst of night nursing, the oxytocin rush of letting milk. My body was becoming mine again. The coursing heat, interrupting and dizzying, lasted more than a year. I had a spinal tap when a brain MRI couldn't rule out multiple sclerosis. I was told I did not have MS and would probably not develop it later. What I had, and have, are three mysterious lesions on my brain. "Nothing conclusive, but enough to form a pattern," the neurologist said. The lesions could be a physical reminder of past migraines or the mark of toxic encephalopathy caused by exposure to lead, building materials, or pesticides that diffuse into the brain; they are lipophilic and cross the blood-brain barrier.

My brain was a lit night sky on the neurologist's computer screen. Pit mine from satellite. Two systems should not have merged but had, and one had violated and polluted another. All that year, I wanted to escape my body. I could not escape my body.

The Long Night

The harm dragged on, spilled, emptied, but first day slipped into humid night and the seventy-two-car freight train moved northeast from North Dakota carrying nearly eight million liters of shale oil up into Canada, where the driver stopped for the night to rest in town, where all the rail yard attendants left the yard to sleep, where later, the unsecured tank cars moved as if waking, breached and derailed and exploded, killing forty-seven people in Lac-Mégantic.

It was supposed to be just a stopover for the eight million liters of shale oil that night; the town, by then, was used to trains hauling Bakken Formation crude, the transitory constancy and dull rumblings. It was Saturday, around one in the morning in the city of nearly six thousand. Music from downtown pubs lifting over those who were still out, bare-armed and smoking and dancing.

The disaster destroyed more than thirty buildings. Lac-Mégantic decided to flatten the still-contaminated downtown, which had continued to soak oil after the crash: six million liters, what hadn't gone up in flames. Wrecked but not destroyed, some of the Lac-Mégantic businesses impacted by proximity to the crash opened their doors for the eight hours before they were set to be flattened.

Some chose to visit sections of their downtown, see shop owners they were on friendly terms with, in a gesture of collective
mourning.

Other gestures like this would come later: galleries, on the anni-
versary, showed floor-to-ceiling framed photographs of the town
and its citizens before the derailment. There were consequences
of trauma. From a mental health study conducted in town after
the crash: 25 percent of the children surveyed showed symptoms
of post-traumatic stress disorder, and the rate among adults was
50 percent; 39 percent of teenagers had suicidal thoughts, a rate
twice the Quebec average. Solidarity and the pain of grief rose up
in the days and months and years after the town was thrust into
immediate and communal violence. A plurality of death, night of
terror, a cruel night. People who loved each other and loved this
place absorbed all that they had so suddenly lost together.

This wasn't any grief; it was oil grief; it was capital grief.

In their night sky installation, *Black Shoals Stock Market
Planetarium,* London-based artists Lise Autogena and Joshua
Portway projected starlight on the inner sphere of a dome. They
placed beanbags underneath, where viewers could lean back and

look up. The constellations did not reflect suns or planets but instead publicly traded companies: a computer program turned the live financial activity of the world's stock exchanges into stars. The market slumped and the bright lights faded; a good day of trading, and the stars shined brightly. When I look up at night I see stars and planets, airplanes and satellites, astral bodies and industry; sometimes I cannot tell the real from the manufactured. The artists' installation imitates the co-opting of nature for corporate financial gain, critiquing the long capitalist history of colonizing and transgressing people and environments.

The night sky installation hides the market that controls the sky. It performs an obfuscation. After the train derailment, three men sat trial—a train driver and engineer, a man in charge of rail circulation, and a manager of train operations—but not railway executives. It was wrong that they were the only ones to sit trial, and incomplete. How many lines of blame should be followed like track after such a violence? How wide is the reach of this disaster?

My friend Gudrun says, while we walk our dogs through our neighborhood, "It's the same violence here. Just a matter of time before one of these trains derails." Around us, tankers full of liquified petroleum gas rumble past. The black cylinders are sleek as stones. There are fifty, there are one hundred, there are so many that I lose count while we walk our dogs the zigzagging blocks.

For the length of time I've lived here, seven years, I have admired the community gardens on our walks. These spaces aren't grids of single-family homes with fenced yards and racist covenant–laced pasts but instead a kind of visual abundance: good-smelling flowers, vines dripping fruit. For the relatively modest price of water, under one hundred dollars a year, anyone can plant here. So people come to grow.

Many community gardens in Minneapolis are located on throwaway slivers of corporate-owned grass. Beside Shoreham Yards sits the Shoreham Community Garden. The garden over in Marshall Terrace, with good free mulch, is on land owned by Xcel Energy. Brown, leaf-strewn mounds, trees gone to mulch, face the imposing Riverside Generating Plant, a combined-cycle powerplant on the banks of the Mississippi River built first as a coal station and later converted to natural gas. Just offshore from the plant, a noisy heron rookery has overtaken a slip of river island.

When I walk by these gardens I see people of various races and genders and ages planting, and sometimes we wave to each other. Gentrification is evident here, tall condos sprouting up along the rail yards and the river, but the gardens seem to me to hold a different potential, evidence of a different ecological relationship with place.

Perhaps they are closer to what bell hooks writes about in her essay "Again—Segregation Must End" on the culture of places where care can be seen on full display. Hooks writes, "Those of us who truly believe racism can end, that white supremacist thought and action can be challenged and changed, understand that there is an element of risk as we work to build community across difference. The effort to build community in a social context of racial inequality (much of which is class based) requires an ethic of relational reciprocity, one that is anti-domination. . . . Living in a community where many citizens work to end domination in all forms, including racial domination, a central aspect of our local culture is a willingness to be of service."

I see the gardens as anti-domination; places where people come together across difference to be of service to soil.

One day, I get a call from Evie, the garden manager. My name has risen to the top of her waitlist. A plot is open, and do I want it?

What I want is to be in a better ecological relationship with where I live. I imagine growing tomatoes on the rail yard's property and then placing a sign by the vines that reads, "Free, please take." I wonder if what I could grow from this brownfield, despite my intentions, would hold chemicals at high concentrations in fruit and vegetable skins. If what I could grow would sicken.

The complexity of good plants growing in polluted soil is something that Mary Siisip Geniusz writes about in *Plants Have So Much to Give Us, All We Have to Do Is Ask,* her book of Anishinaabe botanical teachings written with both Native and non-Native gardeners in mind. On the potential medicinal dangers of picking roadside mullein, Geniusz writes that, with slime molds being the one exception, "Plants cannot get up and move. . . . Because they cannot move, they are forced to take up whatever is in the soil where they are growing. If good things are in the soil, they soak up good things. If poisons are in the soil, they have to take up the poisons."

On a bright October day, I meet Evie in the garden. We walk through rows of beans and hefty late-season blooms. She tells me how long she's been gardening here, two years, and as we walk she pauses to pluck tomatoes from the vines lining her plot. My purse swells with green zebras, tomatillos, purple-stalked kale. She is kind in a way that overwhelms me. We wear masks. The COVID-19 pandemic surges and it has been many months since I've walked through a garden with anyone. Slow-moving trains behind the chain-link at Shoreham push on, slate black against the sky.

This garden has thirty sunny plots, she says, as we pass tarped topsoil underneath the shade of apple and cherry trees. I ask who else gardens here. "Many of the garden plots are leased by first-generation immigrants," she says. "They've been gardening these plots for twenty-odd years." When she posts signs about issues pertinent to the garden on the wooden community board at the center of the maze of plots—a note about the all-garden fence-building day, a reminder not to use pesticides—she posts them in six languages, including Ukrainian. Three generations of Ukrainian gardeners grow over several plots, she tells me.

It's chilly as we walk and talk voles and mice and potato tubers. A few other gardeners are out, watering and weeding. She waves and they wave back. When she points to a patch of chernobyl, I repeat back the word, surprised to be saying it here, and she smiles. "I've learned the Ukrainian word for lots of plants. I mean mugwort. See that bunch there?"

The Chernobyl Nuclear Power Plant derives its name from the Ukrainian word for mugwort, a black-stalked, clump-forming perennial. In 1986, when a nuclear accident occurred at the No. 4

reactor in the Chernobyl Nuclear Power Plant near the city of Pripyat in the north of the Ukrainian SSR, it launched the word *chernobyl* out of the realm of garden perennials and into the linguistic arena of synonym, shorthand for ruin. *Chernobyl* now means "toxic" and has become inextricable from one of the worst nuclear disasters in history.

To say "chernobyl" in the garden, though we are merely discussing the presence of mugwort, feels like speaking in prescient metaphor.

I tell Evie that my own ancestry is partly Ukrainian Jews. That it might be nice to learn plant names in Ukrainian, were I to garden here next spring.

Behind us, crude tankers cut the horizon. The sun is beginning to set over them.

I think of Camille T. Dungy's ecotones, a diversity of systems edging up against each other. This garden that sits above a polluted groundwater aquifer and shares a fence line with decades of industry.

I ask Evie if she knows why so many community gardens around us are on corporate land, and she laughs back and says, "What isn't owned by the railroads in this neighborhood?" I ask if she's worried about soil toxicity—if this soil has ever been tested for arsenic, volatile organic compounds, lead. She shrugs and her cheeks bunch behind her mask in a polite smile, "I'm not *all* knowing." I dig my hands into my coat pockets and worry a hole at the bottom of one side. I stick my finger into the lining where there's the outline of wool and then nothing. My questions about the rail yard and its toxic legacy feel pretentious and academic in the garden.

I leave with no answers but tell her I'd like to water, plant, and tend a plot here next spring; I leave with Evie's gifts. Hefty tomatoes, delicate lantern-skinned tomatillos, basil. Bunched on my car's passenger seat, the green and purple bounty is glossy as velvet and looks terribly delicious in the day's dying light.

Dredge

Gudrun wants to plant a forest next to the playground and public garden where, over the fence, oil tankers move in a sleek constant line.

She's thinking bigger than a copse, more like the several hundred poplars they've got near the baseball fields and U.S. Navy ponds and landfills next to Moffett Field, the Superfund outside San Francisco.

The trees suck carcinogens out of the 1,500-acre site through their roots, soak up fifty gallons of toxic water a day and break it down into carbon dioxide and chloride. No excavating, no dredging to decontaminate. The poplars, as a result of human manipulation, are cut with a microbe that helps the trees break down the solvents and degreasers they absorb.

Nothing here is dead yet, I remind myself, though it is all damaged. I think I'll plant some of her forest. I'd like to dig a hole into this ground and fill it with something alive.

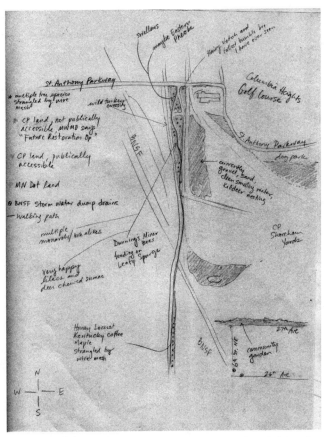

Illustration of Shoreham Yards by Gudrun Lock, Minneapolis, Minnesota.

From: Gudrun Lock

Soo Line Shoreham Yards Brownfield/VIC Site, Minnesota

Here the air smells like diesel smoke. There's a black snake of oil cars moving through this neighborhood all day and all night long.

Encountering Shoreham Yards was a slow process for me, moving here fourteen years ago, I smelled it but didn't know what it was. Like a lot of industrial places and similar sites within cities, I think we're always sort of aware that they're there, because we sense them. Even without knowing exactly what they are or do, we can feel them vibrating the ground.

Two blocks from my house is Shoreham Yards. I walk my dog along a path that runs beside it, through a grassy buffer lining the fence, separating us. There's a community garden at one end and a scrappy playground for kids at the other where I used to take my boys. I always noticed lots of trucks and shipping containers, noise and exhaust fumes, across the fence.

I started to pay attention to all the different ecologies here. I started to see more of the landscape, the soil, and the complexity of all of us living on this polluted edge.

The idea to revitalize the area began after I watched a film. It was about this botanist who claims to be a descendent of Druids. It made me nostalgic in a very specific way; I remembered who I was when I was seven years old. Because when I was little, like a lot of young people, I thought that I could communicate with trees and rocks and water. It seemed so obvious to me. But our culture basically told me to shut up and to stop thinking that way, because it was childish or fantastical or ridiculous.

Watching this film—it was about how trees communicate underground, keep water systems healthy, store carbon, the chemicals they release, and the ways people feel when they're around trees because of the aerosols they produce—the film gave me a kind of permission to start thinking in that way again about trees. Seeing them as beings with their own needs; seeing them as communicative and relational.

The next morning when I walked my dog along Shoreham, I had the thought: *a forest should be here.*

I got curious; read public documents. Thousands of pages and reams and reams of data sets about things like chlorinated solvents and pentachlorophenol. I learned the yard is a Voluntary Investigation and Cleanup site, like a Superfund, except the business is still active.

Voluntary Investigation and Cleanup connects the company with the state pollution control agency to help clean up without risk of litigation. It sounds so innocuous, doesn't it? The language suggests that the rail company is doing it out of the goodness of their hearts, when in fact, they are required to by law if that level of toxicity is present.

A business that used to rent land on Shoreham Yards stored chemicals underground that leaked into the groundwater system for the whole neighborhood. If, or really *when*, an oil train car tips into the Mississippi River, fowling our city's drinking water, we won't be able to tap into our groundwater like other neighborhoods will be able to do. Our water will have to be driven in by truck or something.

Lately, I've been thinking about the psychological effects of this place. I see a lack of imagination, a kind of violence, and a sense deprivation reflected back. You know, there's garbage in the ditch, trees hacked by the electric company or park board, so little beauty, and a feeling of disconnectedness from the living systems around us. The Soo Line Dump contains plastic, glass, metal, brick, concrete, wood, ash, tar, coal, alkaline batteries, arsenic, cadmium, lead, mercury.

Some days, I go birding in the mornings over there.

Every time I walk the dump, I see what has been abused and used for all kinds of different things. It doesn't even know what it is anymore, this polluted place, and of course I'm anthropomorphizing, but that's the way it feels to me.

I think what's on the surface speaks to what's underneath. The soil is one way of measuring history and time, how the transitions of the land and its uses have laid themselves down in the ground. Geological time can be seen in maps showing the movement of polluted groundwater. Some buffers of Shoreham are rich in pollinators and organic matter; others are almost blank. "Fill" has been laid on top of historic pollution. All of this—the surface and what's underneath—continues to make and remake. So it's interesting to me to think about what cleanup entails. The rail company says, *We've done everything we're supposed to, we cleaned up that chemical spill, cleaned up the degreaser spill, cleaned up those old tires, rail ties, and asbestos shingles,* but what actually does that mean? Where does the soil go to next? Buried and contained below or carted off? Becoming some other community's problem?

I think, like a lot of people, I mostly spent the early years I lived in this neighborhood walking in the opposite direction of Shoreham. Intermodal train, trucking, and distribution sites are about exclusion, extraction, financial capital, right? They are not about living systems. Business is the priority, and it's very clear that that's the priority. You can smell that that's the priority. The dust in the air is not for me to breathe.

So I think all those things were in me subconsciously for a long time.

Realistically, the train yard isn't going away. This pollution is here. It exists and continues in one form or another, whether they've cleaned it up to EPA standards or not. So what do we do now? How to imagine other kinds of time frames? Other scales; what lives in the soil; what does that tree want; what does winter mean for the badger who lives there? If I look for long enough and try to think about the perspective a tree might have and how it might be speaking with things underground—I'm thinking about bacteria and fungi, nematodes, also down there with the buried sludge and concrete and creosote railroad ties. I am thinking of trees having their very own conversations, really, about their own needs, that have absolutely fuck all to do with us, then I wonder how trees become central to the conversation without me necessarily centering myself in the process, you know?

I'm aware of the pitfalls of idealizing this whole situation. Regardless, my point is that the nonhuman world has its own interests and no one can live without them. The birds and trees are not going to abide by human desires; they have their own thing going on.

You know, that reminds me of something. At Shoreham, over by the dump, there are all these wild sunflowers, which are phytoremediator plants; they extract and remove pollutants. The sunflowers take up heavy metals and stabilize them, keeping them out of soil and water systems. I wonder what is growing there now that is an antidote to extraction and self-centeredness and our death cult of consumerism? I wonder if it's pushing through the ground as we speak, patiently creating another world, not waiting to find out if we people want one or not.

Decay Theory

At a lecture on archive theory I'm drawn to the theories of decay.
The archivist preserves ephemera from shuttered gay nightclubs.
Mildewed matchbooks or patches of barstool vinyl. Ephemera and
decay theory counter dominant narratives about whose history
matters and why, the archivist says. Such ephemeral preservation
calls attention to what has been called "trash" and who has deemed
it such, exposing the limits and prejudices of the archives.

The archivist then asks us to consider the stakes in our preserving—
What do you keep, and why? What if the archive doesn't want you?
What if what you keep wants to disappear? What if your preserving is
an act of greed?

In the Hospital

Before some scans, my father had radioactive glucose injected, then waited by himself in a room for one hour. For that hour, he was radioactive too.

The pamphlet reads: *Do not hold children in your lap until the radioactive sweetness is gone.* It was March going into April. Safe radioactive sugar. To find tumors spread throughout his body.

In the science of decay, radioactive elements can decay suddenly. Spontaneous fission happens when a large unstable nucleus splits in two.

The primary element in the life of such an isotope is called the parent. The product is called the daughter.

But this isn't a story about my body.

The questions we started to voice on the phone: Would it be O.K. for me to bring his grandson to his apartment after school, or would he, by then, still be too full of radioactive elements?

Anne Carson writes, "It is as if we have all been lowered into an atmosphere of glass." We entered a terrarium.

In the hospital, I take notes on my cell phone that say: *Spleen, pancreas, right kidney—okay. Left kidney, cyst maybe? Space between liver and stomach, more fluid. New fluid? Single lymph node between the lungs is prominent.*

Between his treatments and tests, I take the elevator to different floors. I recognize a mother from my son's elementary school and we say hello. She's on her way to a different hospital floor, to deliver a baby.

Driving home, I start buying lottery tickets. Scratch-offs. Winner Winner Chicken Dinner. Luck.

During his treatments, I read a book about volcanoes in the hospital. Read about tectonic and volcanic areas, rift zones, main lateral volcanic belts. Read about fracture zones, areas of transformed lineaments, grabens. I underline a passage: *The mantle plume disappears under the new Iceland, the island grows and its oldest parts become eroded and disappear below sea level.*

A rifting is the splitting apart of a tectonic plate. Rifting can be violent and subterranean. A fracture zone, a scar on the seafloor caused by the split. His rifting body—he was erupting and eroding. He would disappear.

He does not buy new clothes to die in. He wears the clothes he wore when he was healthy and they become like dress-up clothes on a child. After he stops working, his jeans still show evidence from jobsites, and the suit he wore to church to attend his father's funeral is ten sizes too large. His cheeks and neck are sallow and concave but he smiles at relatives at the reception, and his smile points forward to death and back to the man he was the last time they saw him grin.

He tells his siblings that he doesn't snore anymore, which is some victory. They act impressed, and he says, "I quit smoking and lost forty pounds, that must be why, but I wouldn't recommend my diet." We wince smiles to hide knowing that it is seventy pounds. He can't eat anymore.

One night, my boyfriend has weed mints. I eat too much of what he's lucked into. We sit on his balcony. I don't feel like anyone's mother or anyone's daughter, just this brief body. Legs dusted with streetlights. I might as well be soil. Then I am salt-sweat tears. Maybe I'm eroding.

Love Canal, a neighborhood in Niagara Falls, New York, became infamous in the 1970s as a landfill-turned-community where kids were poisoned in their homes. The town was built on a heap of toxic waste—the town a former dump site for the city of Niagara Falls and then the Hooker Chemical Company. So frustrated with the federal government's lackluster response to this emergency, enraged by the reports of chromosome damage in their children, two residents of Love Canal held EPA agents hostage.

Lois Gibbs, partly responsible for the EPA hostage situation, was described in a retrospective profile piece as "so shy at the start of the struggle she tried to hide behind a tree when neighbors called on her."

The government's failures to address the public health concerns expressed by New York's Love Canal residents led people to the point of rocking cars in the streets, pouring gasoline on their lawns to spell out *EPA,* and lighting the letters on fire.

Before this, Lois knocked on doors, learned about her neighbors' children's illnesses. Sons with asthma; daughters with epilepsy, kidney failure. Stones thrown against rough concrete sparked. One afternoon, a child was severely burned when rocks he'd gathered in his pocket caught fire from the friction he made running. There was more: the EPA issued a study showing that the chemicals found in the Love Canal area could cause genetic damage in later generations. Grandchildren in a far future, in another place, could still be sickened.

In the aftermath of these discoveries, the federal Superfund trust was established by Congress in 1980 to pay for the cleanup of abandoned toxic waste sites. Gibbs is affectionately called the Mother of the Superfund because her activism got Love Canal noticed by President Carter. Through a mother's activism, the questions I myself ask now, about the interplay of bodies and places and generations, echo across time and distances.

Since the Superfund attempts to cover costs for remediating abandoned toxic sites, the fund defines what constitutes an "environment" and a "release" in legal language.

Under section 101(22) of CERCLA, a release means any "spilling, leaking, pumping, pouring, emitting, emptying, discharging, injecting, escaping, leaching, dumping, or disposing into the environment." This release could be immediate or gradual.

At the hospital, my father was always leaking, emptying, and parts of his body were dumped, disposed of, and sometimes he was so weak from all this that I would hold my arm out, and he would balance on me to stand.

His stomach was cut in half because one half was eaten through with cancer, his surgeon explained. "The stomach is big," he said. "It's like he had two stomachs before and now he has one."

"Half a stomach," I correct.

"That is true too," he said.

"Whatever you do, make a little video of him on your phone," my friend, who'd lost her father to lung cancer the year before, had advised. "Just him moving around the way he does. Him being himself." I never made a video and then it was too late. I tried once at his apartment, while we were organizing his bookshelf together, but it felt too invasive to record him performing his living for me, which was also to record him performing his dying.

One day, his oncologist used the word *remission*. I was stunned. My father grinned like he'd won the lottery. His oncologist was showing us his latest CT results. On her computer monitor were his lungs and liver, kidneys and digestive tract. Gray and black and white images, blurry and abstracted flesh and fluids. I had adjusted to invading him, injecting my eyes. The screen helped with this crossing, made his body a double, a real and unreal thing, or a new body.

Each image on-screen was named body; they were always named body. What strange giddiness crept through the room, watching. It was like he was pregnant and we were excited. She showed us his tumor, the fluid that moated around it. Today there was less tumor, more fluid; this was maybe good.

It wasn't a casual relationship I formed with the lottery that year, but a compulsion. Daily. Always single-dollar scratch-offs. Many of them. The two-dollar wins hooked me. Just slightly better than nothing.

After his stomach ruptured again, suddenly and painfully, there was a leaking sink in his ICU room, and it pissed him off. Someone had come to fix it during the day, but they did a poor job, and by evening it was leaking again. If he could stand, if he had his tools, it would be a simple fix. He was high on morphine and itching to do the job himself. But his stomach was surgically opened. He was strung through with tubes and could not speak, only write. So I asked how he would fix the sink. On a yellow legal pad, he wrote the tools required, the steps, methodically, relishing every detail. I had come to the hospital after teaching a college composition course where the semester's students were especially generous with their work and with each other. I watched him write out the steps to fix the leaking sink, my father who made his living with his body. Now here was language, this thin approximation of living, stitching us.

Between treatments he leaks. It's weeks or months, but no matter who fixed him, he opens again. His stomach ruptures and acid flows internally, damaging his surrounding organ tissue. His cancer is full of bodily violence, bodily eruptions.

Volcanoes have long been appropriated into human narratives, likened to destruction or desire. During the French revolution, eruption was a popular metaphor to mobilize revolutionaries—*éruption!*

To study a volcano, to predict large eruptions, geologists measure small earthquakes that happen inside and around the volcano. If pressure increases in a volcano, it produces little earthquakes, and the more pressure on a volcano, the more little earthquakes in that volcano. This slow breakdown of stability inside the volcano is what produces the big eruptions. I read this in the volcano book I lug in my purse to the hospital and think how human, how disappointingly human.

All that year, holes in his GI tract leaching acid, éruption!

I begin to think about environments that don't behave, flesh that won't stay put, what spills, what leaks, what opens, what revolts.

On the day Stephen Paddock opened fire on a crowd of concertgoers from the thirty-second-floor luxury suite of the Las Vegas Mandalay Bay Resort and Casino, my father's oncologist explained that his bone marrow was too weak, his white blood cell count too low, to continue with further treatment. His body was not strong enough to fight even a bacterial skin infection. She skated her fingers along her forearm to demonstrate busy bacteria and I skated my fingers along my forearm and imagined what lived on me. My father closed his eyes and said, "O.K., all right," sounding so tired. His billowy jeans fell around his shoes in folds like a skirt.

The news that day played, and I could hear it inside the hospital's maroon-walled financial aid office.

He was lucky, my father, in his way, because he was the right age to die poor in this country, on the cusp of his sixty-sixth birthday. Lucky because he was able to access Medicaid benefits and gap health insurance coverage, privately, in the state where we lived, and lucky because the Affordable Care Act meant that a man like him, without insurance, could be insured after diagnosis.

I became his body's proxy on hold lines, in government buildings, like other children of parents uninsured but able to access societal privilege through citizenship status and so able to fall into America's biomedical cancer system. "Does he have any assets?" the financial aid officer had asked me. "Because those will be seized." "No," I said back, "he owns nothing of value." I remember feeling relieved for him when I explained what little he owned.

The air in the hospital was diffuse with suffering. The news pumped the horror coming from Nevada. "We thought it was fireworks," people interviewed said, when asked to describe the moment before they understood.

"Hello, again," my father says to a corner of the room after an operation. High, hallucinating, seeing ghosts. It wasn't just anyone he saw but his dead mother, he tells me, grinning back. It was relieving, to imagine his death as a reunion. A big summer barbeque stretching into evening with music and laughter.

There are other notes on my cell phone that say things like: *Our yard full of solar panels, extra awnings, stacked lumber, PVC pipe, generators, just in case, someday.*

On his sixty-sixth birthday, I go to the grocery store and buy him a newspaper and a pile of food he didn't ask for and can't eat along with the 7Up he wanted. I buy myself Winner Winner Chicken Dinner.

Edwidge Danticat, writing about her mother's death from cancer, observes that after her mother died, she read the Bible's Book of Revelation. "Mixing history and prophecy, Revelation, with its fiery forecasts of famines, earthquakes, plagues, and wars, is filled with apocalyptic fury. . . . It is the one book I kept returning to in the early days after my mother died."

For Danticat, it felt odd to be drawn to such violent imagery, and it was also odd for me to be pulled toward volcanoes, earthquakes, environmental ruin, Superfunds, and brownfields, all this ruin porn. Daily, I rubbernecked industrial parks. I felt lit inside.

Out the sliding glass door of the apartment he rented now to be close to his treatment there was one chair and a table that would have held an ashtray and pack of Marlboro Lights in a different year. For weeks, he'd been vomiting he said, but he was still hungry. Food sounded delicious. He'd watch hours of cooking shows on TV. Pull over beside the road, driving to chemo, to vomit. Next to the TV, there was a blue box with his dormant tools and his handwriting on it, *plum bing,* a little space between the letters, and below, a different box marked *fragile. Plum bing, fragile.* We sat next to each other in two recliners and watched a sappy movie about a woman who kept falling out of love.

At home, my eight-year-old wanted only to play Monopoly, because it was the game he would play with his grandpa.

One night, I snapped at him and said, "I cannot play that game tonight because it is capitalist propaganda," and his eyes went to his feet in swift shame. His grief was raw and I was being idiotic. He wanted a game, a fantasy where he was powerful, had places to go and money to spend. Where all chance was good chance, or at least the bad luck was solvable. Where jail was an equal risk for all players regardless of who they were, easy to leave; where there was a chest called community, a free parking lot that sometimes paid you; where bank errors only benefitted players. I apologized and brought out the board.

After the Howe chemical fire, sediment was trucked off as waste— clay, silt, sand, gravel, deeper earth materials than soil, dug up and taken away. Groundwater was pumped for six months before the pumping stopped, and a decade later, a portion of the scarred earth was paved for use as a storage lot for semitrailers.

Factories along the Mississippi River smelled bad, and I knew I was close to home before I could read the freeway exit signs by the heavy air, dense with cooling asphalt.

Shingles factories are shutting down in Mobile, Alabama, and in Minneapolis, residents in the neighborhoods that surround the Lowry Avenue Bridge and the GAF Shingle Factory want the factory gone. Community research and organizing have exposed decades of toxic pollution in the air of North and Northeast Minneapolis. The state pollution control agency has studied the air around my childhood neighborhood because its residents experience a higher rate of asthma and cancer than those who don't live near the river bank of factories.

In a 1975 National Cancer Institute study, air pollution was seen as possibly contributing to the higher death rate for stomach cancer in Minnesota. For the state as a whole, the death rate for stomach cancer, in that year, was 20 percent above the national average.

He bought the house in 1994. It was listed in the paper's real estate section for a price of $31,000.

Once he bought the house, I was single-minded in my desire that he get a dog.

Soon we had Lady, a bushy West Highland terrier. A woman whose townhome he was remodeling off-loaded her onto us because she barked too much for her housing association.

I was thrilled and loved Lady endlessly. She slept in my bed every night, in the home's single bedroom. My father snoring on the living room couch.

My childhood neighborhood is kempt now, popular with my friends. Flowering gardens, a new grocery, a new library building, and a public plant-filtered pool. When I talk to people I know who have just moved there to raise families, there is an awkwardness I feel because I never mention legacy pollution, only that I was raised there, too, and how good it was. This is not a lie, though it is incomplete.

In a 1960 public health study, it was found that "the higher the index of air pollution (from industry, automobiles, and heating), the higher the death rate in these four areas: cancer of the esophagus and stomach; cancer of the trachea, bronchus, and lung; heart disease and hardening of the arteries; chronic endocarditis (inflammation of the heart lining)."

I wonder what disease I will get and who will keen for me when I do.

I was nine when my father moved us next to that Superfund. My son was five when I moved him next to this brownfield. If this were a work of fiction, that would be the kind of odd symmetry that would put readers off. It would seem too neat, too coincidental.

I tell this to a friend who kindly laughs back and says, "Wouldn't it be the opposite?" Wouldn't it be the more unbelievable thing if I were able to get away? Isn't that one way that oppression works? The coincidence would be in the escape.

In her elegy for her brother, Anne Carson writes, "I wanted to fill my elegy with light of all kinds. But death makes us stingy. There is nothing more to be expended on that, we think, he's dead. Love cannot alter it. Words cannot add to it. No matter how I try to evoke the starry lad he was, it remains a plain, odd history. So I began to think about history."

I wanted history. I wanted sediment, geologic time, earth.

Through a mutual friend, I become acquainted with soil scientist Nic Jelinski, who teaches me things about groundwater plumes and aquafers. Aquafers can encompass multiple watersheds. Soil plays a critical role in mediating water quality. With groundwater pollution, chemicals can be released into the air. Aquafers are in porous materials. Sandstone. City soils can be both fertile and have contamination; this makes them hearty and biodiverse but easy to overlook as valuable from a planting or microbial perspective. The science is moving toward understanding the whole system, he says. In fence-line environments, we've touched everything. Soil is what we also are, which is something he loves about it. "If you think about it, all our bodies are only briefly not soil."

The suit was brought in 1977, and the Lloyd A. Fry Roofing Company agreed to pay the state for pollution-control violations. Fry had been violating air-quality standards for over a decade at the plant by the home where I slept each night with Lady and learned to jelly rhubarb stalks. The Fry plant produced shingles and other asphalt products.

The soil and groundwater had long been contaminated by the time we moved in, with diesel-range organics and semivolatile organic compounds, with polyaromatic hydrocarbons, pesticides, grease, and motor oil.

In 1956, residents by the rail yard held an outdoor meeting to protest switching operations. The rail line had outgrown its facilities and the company was even talking about expanding the switching yard. The residents complained of "heavy, all-night switching."

The precise ways bodies are harmed by exposure to toxicity is notoriously difficult to track. Proving this harm can require decades, if it is proven at all. So it is hard for advocates to serve justice to bodies harmed by polluted ecologies. In places where exposures persist, their persistence and its link to disease and thus corporate culpability and redress can make for a steep and ambiguous uphill battle. Why do some get sick, and others don't?

Nevertheless, Rachel Carson knew when she was writing *Silent Spring*, the years she was dying from breast cancer, that "there is also an ecology of the world within our bodies." Bodies are places in the least hyperbolic terms. Bodies are environments, even if the law's language, written to protect our bodies from what harms them in our environments, is ineffective.

In 1896, the *American Journal of Psychology* reported that earthquakes and drowning were feared more than cancer, seen by many as more threatening to human life. In Oklahoma, where the man

I love lives, most new earthquakes since fracking are caused by wastewater disposal, a related process. Fluid waste from oil and gas production is injected deep below groundwater aquifers. From 2014 to 2017, a surge in seismicity caused more earthquakes in Oklahoma than California.

Oil and gas industries are exempted from sections of the Clean Air Act, the Safe Drinking Water Act, and the federal Superfund. They pose dangers but enjoy a freedom that is so like being born a man or white or wealthy in this society. The harm is real, yet suffered by others.

Maybe oil and gas exemptions are to blame for the situation in Dish, Texas. In Dish, population 225, people are sick at such a volume they are having blood and urine tested for toxins, but environmental epidemiologists have struggled to articulate precisely how the swift changes caused by the fracking industry and their illnesses intertwine. Gas wells and heavy equipment ring Dish, a town that won a bid to be renamed after the TV provider in exchange for free satellite service. Solid tumors can take 20 years after chemical exposure to develop, and links between a type of cancer and a chemical known to cause it need to be airtight before they're considered proven.

When I was a kid and accompanied my dad on weekend service calls, he always told me that you should never park in the driveway. If you want another call, he reasoned, you shouldn't block the professor's Lexus.

Now I joke with him at the hospital, "Dad, professors don't drive fancy cars."

Some do, he insists. "Fine," I correct myself. "If I limit my point to adjunct faculty, I'm still right."

"You always like being right." He spits into a cup and asks me to wet his mouth with the small green sponge that I can dip into water and place on his tongue. He is not allowed to drink anymore, just permitted this sponge. He smiles when the cool water hits his chapped lips. It must feel so good. Maybe it is the only thing that feels good now.

Gertrude Stein died of stomach cancer. She said, "if everybody did not die the earth would be all covered over and I, I as I, could not have come to be and try as much as I can try not to be I, nevertheless, I would mind that so much, as much as anything, so then why not die, and yet and again not a thing, not a thing to be liking, not a thing."

From my father's patient-visit summaries and health records: "Technique: Images were obtained through the chest, abdomen, and pelvis."

Findings, chest: "There are new small ill-defined nodular groundglass opacities in the inferior right upper lobe which have a centrilobular distribution on series three, images thirty-six through forty-nine."

I thought it was a subjunctive idea, his oncologist explaining groundglass to me: an area of increased attenuation due to air displacement by fluid. A finding that isn't meaning. "Is it more cancer?" I had asked. She said, "No, not exactly." Groundglass only suggests itself. Ill-defined small swell of cells. A hazy opacity resisting interpretation.

He used to point out the stars to me at night. They looked like flints of chalk on a chalkboard. Bright marks in stark relief against everything.

In photography, a sheet of groundglass is useful for manual focusing. With a groundglass viewer inserted in the back of some large cameras, the image appears upside down, in vivid detail. Groundglass, frosted on lamp fixtures, dimming the bulb beneath. And in an optical microscope, groundglass illuminates the field behind the specimen. He is the specimen; we take him in. The opacities send light across the field behind his body, which is history. He's made of a milky dust, diesel exhaust, mosaic of blood and heat. His lungs fill her computer monitor with a galaxy.

All that year, his stomach opening. He'd leak. Poor plumbing, he'd joke. Then they'd open him in the ICU. Drain him. Again, an NG tube. A pump. A plastic receptacle filling with his body's red fluids.

Anne Boyer: "Everything we were supposed to keep inside of us now seems to fall out. Blood from chemotherapy-induced nosebleeds drips on the sheets, the paperwork, the CVS receipts, the library books. We can't stop crying. We emit foul odors. We throw up. We have poisonous vaginas and poisoned sperm. Our urine is so toxic that the signs in the bathroom instruct patients to flush twice."

What is inside comes out. What is outside comes in.

Does This Cause Cancer? Acrylamide / Agent Orange / Alcohol / Antiperspirants / Arsenic / Asbestos / Aspartame / Benzene / Bovine Growth Hormone / Cellular Phones / Cellular Towers / Cosmetics / Diesel Exhaust / Electrical Devices / Formaldehyde /

Hair Dyes / Medical Treatment / Microwaves / Perfluorooctanoic Acid / Power Lines / Radio Waves / Radon / Recombinant / Smart Meters / Sun / Talcum Powder / Teflon.

He gets high from the operations, the drugs he's given, and after every operation, he always asks the same thing: "When can we go dancing?" One time I answer back, "Tonight!"

Only once, I win twenty dollars off a single Winner Winner Chicken Dinner, and burst into tears.

"Meet my father," I say to the Oklahoma boyfriend. There he is, all white sheets and tubes, a line of blood draining from his nostrils down to a sort of medical Big Gulp at our feet. I wear nude suede shoes and I don't want to mess them with his blood and immediately feel ashamed.

When my son was breastfeeding, I also didn't want to get any of myself on myself, but I was always leaking, always opening. The damp milk-heat was tautness, rush, and life.

What is the difference between opening to let life in and opening to let life out? Maybe it is only the smells bodies make and what is confessed by them.

I've been to Iceland once. I swam their famous pools. Took on the scent of the water on my skin, a metallic, mineral smell. Sulphur, clay. After, I felt feral, less domesticated, far from my son, less recognizable to myself, smelling of the soil of an ecosystem to which I did not belong.

Chemotherapy changes the body's smell too. Over time my father smelled like a different man. Metallic. The oldest parts of how we'd communicate—his hoisting me up in the air as a baby, or sitting silent on long drives in his truck smelling like cigarettes and gas station coffee, sweaty from jobsites—eroded and disappeared.

For three straight weeks, the doctors say, "Your father's stomach is still open. This way, we can clean him out again." This has something to do with his jaundice, something to do with his sepsis. Their tones were hard to read, some on his rotation struck me as serious, others seemed nearly exclamatory, curious—were his doctors pleased by this? Were they alarmed, but glad to be able to do the cleaning? Years before, he'd taught me how to power hose a deck. I imagined them power hosing his insides.

This one neighbor whom I'm friendly with and who has been organizing against polluters in our neighborhood for decades likes to call Shoreham Yards "our own little Love Canal," by which she means, our scandal, our shared emergency.

But it isn't, not really. It isn't so bad here. It is indeterminately bad, the pollution reports all say, which of course also suggests it is good.

Reading the volcano book again in the hospital, sitting next to a woman in the oncology family lounge, her husband dying from the same kind of cancer killing my father. He was a roofer and had worked with shingles for decades. Laying them down, breathing tar air.

I set the book down and tell the woman in the lounge that I remember a friend of my ex-husband who used to regale us at bars with stories from his medical residency. Things people needed removed from their bodies desperately in the middle of the night. Mostly cell phones vibrating up assholes.

Here we are, waiting for what can't be extracted. In the windowless lounge the woman kicks her shoes off and throws her head back and grins beautifully up to the ceiling. Then she tells me that maybe his job is killing him, but she's glad that they don't live in Mexico anymore, because the cancer treatment he receives here is better.

In the first century, Roman physician Celsus wrote of cancer, its surgical remove, and its aggressive ways, "After excision, even when a scar has formed, nonetheless the disease has returned."

From his medical files, the archives they've become to me, his surgeons wrote: "Patient was prepped and draped in the usual sterile fashion using DuraPrep. We began with a generous upper midline incision and, in the abdomen, encountered murky serosanguineous fluid. This was suctioned out. There was quite a bit of matted small bowel and adhesions. We performed a lysis of adhesions for nearly two hours."

"Eventually, we were able to fire three loads of an Endo-GIA 60 green load across the stomach in order to isolate the gastro-J completely."

"We irrigated the abdomen thoroughly with 6L of sterile water until the effluent ran clear."

I inherited his tools and scraps of sheet metal, plank wood, sinks, toilets he'd pulled off jobsites. Emptying his humid storage locker after his funeral, I recognized that he'd died wanting. He was saving all this to use again, once he was well.

I had thought at times that his refusal to accept his death was shortsighted. I was wrong. It was my job to accept his death, not his. Here I was in his storage shed surrounded by materials that held so much desire for life.

Until the effluent ran clear—in a medical report concerning his body, I read that part again, think about how he could be irrigated. I remembered learning that sometimes whole layers of soil will be hauled off from polluted yards and then new soil hauled in, then the yards replanted; that sometimes, this actually works.

I had the thought standing in his storage locker that sometimes salvage was possible. Salvage wasn't a returning. It was payment for what remained or could be saved after a shipwreck.

On Tenderness

A rail worker at Shoreham Yards keeps an eye out for the owls. Nothing he can do to stop it from happening, really, but some mornings, he sets his work aside to be with the ones found dying near the tracks. After they've hit the tall-stacked shipping containers while hunting through the darkness of the treed and grassy dump in the night.

Psychogeography

I took an interest in aerial maps after I started to walk the margins of polluted, industrial places. From above, I could cross any fence unnoticed.

Geographer Yi-Fu Tuan, writing on how attachments are formed to places, describes "space" as becoming "place" through movement. Walking becomes experience, where meaning and memory are made.

When I walk alone, I am sometimes tracked by security guards; state troopers; men who drive more slowly, roll their car windows down. One day, a woman called out to me as I passed her stoop to be more careful, because I could be raped.

The question of who has the luxury of being unobserved in public space is one of power. I would like to go unnoticed, like a man in Monti Pisani, Italy, who walks chestnut forests that lie in ruin due to a long-running nut industry; overharvesting. He walks to learn how human, animal, and plant communications are "embedded in the forms of living and dead trees." He sketches the ruined forests. Sits alone in the woods for long hours drawing plant disease, tree decay, new growth. He defines his walks and sketches as political acts that encourage the imagining of "different visions of livable futures."

One day, I send a group of first-year college students out of the classroom to walk the campus and record their observations. A young woman of color returns to class with nothing written down. She was followed and harassed. "I couldn't focus," she said. "I was afraid."

"It would be nice, ideal even, if we didn't have to subdivide by gender," Lauren Elkin reflects in her essay *Flâneuse,* on various women's accounts of walking. May-lee Chai, on the emotional labor of movement, and her experiences navigating the intersecting violence of racism and misogyny in public spaces, notes how transgressive walking can be in a world where women have been accused of causing everything from "crop failure" to "their own rapes."

The psychogeography of walking brownfields and Superfunds, the affective aspects of it, lay out the power dynamics that exist, or persist, in a culture. My body, in polluted places, reflects back a terrain where there remains overlap between sexual and ecological forms of violence. These places were built for men, white working men, and seemingly no one else.

Walking, I recall artwork by artist Susanne Slavick, who painted aerials of invented topographies that allude to the female body. The world as body; the body as world. In a series on the political powers enforced by walls and fences, she began to "feminize the graticule, confronting the analytic-rational with the intuitive." In one image, a fence free-floats through the sky, light and prone to movement, able to whip around in the breeze. The houses below are painted with watercolors that run and bleed. The chain-link looks gentle, wafting like a loose feather.

The fence isn't a fence anymore. The protected territory unguarded. I am unguarded on walks; the honey locust trees are unguarded; children in yards, too, plucking cherry tomatoes from vines and placing the fruit, ripe ovary of seeds, on their young tongues.

One day, walking the circumference of the Humboldt Industrial Area, I pass a semitrailer parking lot and a woman alone, dumping. She's parked behind the trailers heaving black construction bags into a dumpster. Next, mildewed drywall she's pulled from the bed of her truck. I respect her dumping and walk more slowly to see what she lifts next. It's Sunday, and it feels like it's just us out here, her dog off leash, rolling in a patch of crabgrass edging the parking lot. Corporations have dumped on this neighborhood for decades. I'd like to think her actions say back, "Fuck off."

Up ahead, another woman on tiptoes in her garden strings a sugar tap for hummingbirds. Her yard is across the street from the Owens Corning roofing plant. Around us, the air smells burdened.

Maybe the woman dumping was returning a violence, shoving her trash in too. May-lee Chai deems this work—of trespass, both imaginative and literal, carried out by women across generations and cultures—vital, "so that our minds [can] be free."

Weeks later, at the Borchert Map Library, housed in a basement room lit with fluorescents at the University of Minnesota, the library director unfurls deep indigo aerials of the industrial area on a table. I have come to see the path I walk from an old sky. Roofs and yards, bluing, edge the chain-link fence where the company-posted Private Property/No Trespassing sign has gone blurry with age. These are images shot from a low-flying plane, the library director tells me, dated to the 1940s. Across the fence I walk alone some days, rail tracks curve and overlap like tangling strands of a necklace forgotten in a drawer. The aerials are blurry. I imagine imprecise crossings. Tree roots tangling. Stormwater running over lead tracks, under fences, down into porous bedrock, down lower, coursing through deep veins of shifting earth.

Bombweed

Saturdays, I dig pepper and blackberry seedlings into loose soil up to my wrists, though sprigs of dill and butter lettuce are all that will return to this brownfield garden plot. What the person here before me grew.

At the garden, I get to thinking about all that fills dark wombs of the earth. Here, dill root; upturned hunks of metal. A man at the garden today is complaining about the recent theft of his garlic scapes. Another plot over, a robust patch of kale is secured by wire and posted warnings. Maybe I have misjudged the communal mood of the garden.

In San Francisco Bay's Bayview-Hunters Point neighborhood, Lindsey Dillon, brownfield scholar, has been studying neighborhood gardens as sites of gentrification and erasure. When she participates in a ground-breaking event at a public lot-turned-community garden, a man who is a new homeowner in the area swings a Weedwacker aggressively and tells her how much he'd like to chop down the smokestack a few blocks away. She writes, "His gesture symbolically severed the emerging present of new development, rising home values, and a whiter residential population from the neighborhood's industrial and racially marginalized past."

For residents in Bayview-Hunters Point, living near one of the nation's most costly brownfield remediation sites, the Hunters Point Naval Shipyard, has caused health consequences—asthma, emphysema, and cancers. Many low-income people were sickened for the length of a century, living beside shipbuilding repair at Hunters Point and the radiological laboratory that operated on the naval base. After the shuttering of the shipyard and a lengthy remediation effort, tall condos were built, which drew a wealthier population. Those who had long lived in the predominantly Black neighborhood were priced out. The celebratory language that coincided with gentrification—calling the area postindustrial and lauding clean-up—are "misnomers that obscure," Dillon observes, historic divestment and structural racism. Brownfield redevelopment rarely benefits the communities who already live there.

The man at the garden wants the smokestack gone. What does it mean when connective tissue between present and past is obscured, erased? "Waste streams through bodies" and soil, Dillon reflects, and so does trauma. How is the grief caused by the "ruins and ruinations of empire" mourned and memorialized when communities affected have been displaced, and physical markers to the past are gone?

My cousin Peter studies *solastalgia,* a term used to describe ecological grief and the mental-health impacts of environmental destruction. *Solastalgia,* mourning for what has been lost to climate catastrophe and what will be lost. He works in the Arizona desert. One day I tell him about my garden plot gone to weeds, and he emails me a paper he's writing on how planting seeds is a self-soothing activity for the climate anxious and ecologically grieving.

I am grieving what is buried in the earth, and by whom. That too often, this burial is a consequence of abuse of power. Closer to my cousin's home in Tempe, the Moab tailings are being moved farther from Arches National Park by rail. For over a decade, the Department of Energy has been moving eleven-million short tons of uranium tailings from Moab to Crescent Junction, Utah, thirty-two miles due north. The relocation is estimated to take another six years to finish. Uranium decays slowly. Plutonium-239 comes from uranium-238 and has a half-life, a daughter nuclei, of twenty-four thousand years.

Leaving a working congress on the rights of future generations and the responsibilities the living hold to them to be "beloved ancestors," writer Rebecca Altman takes a drive to Rocky Flats—the ruins of the northern Denver nuclear weapons plant—before catching her flight home to Boston. Altman doesn't find a sign to mark the history of "what is harbored here, the legacy left in place just below the surface where prairie dogs still burrow." Twenty-four thousand years of radioactive waste concealed, unmarked. "Will future generations know enough to keep looking, to stand guard?" she wonders. Will they know where they are standing when they arrive?

When I drive to Tulsa from Minneapolis, I pass through Kansas City. One day, I take a detour to the Quindaro neighborhood in north Kansas City, Kansas, outside the downtown sprawl with paper mill-turned-condos and pour-over coffee shops. The Quindaro Ruins Archeological Park Project sits on a bluff above the Missouri River dividing Kansas from Missouri. Established around 1857, in the years leading up to the Civil War, Quindaro served as a port of entry for former enslaved people to free-state Kansas.

The ruins were cut off from the rest of Kansas City by the path of the Missouri Pacific Railroad, the Missouri River, and interstate highways, and in 1988, there were city plans to turn them into a landfill, but the Underground Railroad Advisory Commission, Quindaro Town Preservation Society, and Concerned Citizens of Old Quindaro thwarted that effort and helped place Quindaro on the National Register of Historic Places as a historic archaeological district.

On a humid summer day, at the Quindaro Ruins Archeological Park, I stand on a stone platform overlooking the river. Down the bluff, a path leads to the former township. A sign reads, "Quindaro must live on in our hearts, forever." The steps are overgrown with bee balm; the ruins bloom.

I think of bombweed, fireweed. The purple, flowering perennial that returned quickly to World War II bombsites. Sprouting up as if to swallow a landscape desecrated by human actions in new life.

The Old Quindaro Museum needs a new roof. The boarded-up Vernon School, windows smashed. The statue of abolitionist John Brown with its busted fountain. Kansas City–based writer Anne Boyer observes, Quindaro was "an autonomous community built by former enslaved people, indigenous people, and abolitionists, the site at which people who crossed the river could finally be free." It was a community devoted to liberation.

Violet flowers adorn Quindaro. Place of justice, antiracist thought and action, and collective liberation. It is no ruin, but sanctuary forged by revolt. Lively with plant life. When I imagine a landfill here my chest aches.

What might it mean in Bayview-Hunters Point for what grows to signify healing, and not displacement? For fresh food to abundantly feed the community already living there?

At home in the community garden, I question my desire to seed my presence. I like the weeds that quickly return. They are hearty and not trying to mitigate loss or work something out about people and cruelty. By July, the plot has gone to dill and weeds. It's a drought summer. Even if the surface of the garden plays out the usual bullshit—*some strangers, the same sad world*—there's more here rooting, rising.

In Utah's Crescent Junction, the tailings from weapons manufacturing are buried near the joint of Interstate 70 and U.S. Route 191. Tailing planting occurs in phases. First a digging, then a filling. A radon barrier of shale is added, on top of which is laid gravel, soil, and rock. In Crescent Junction, plans are still being made as if stasis should be expected, as if the past can be buried, topped with fill, and forgotten, as if the earth is not shifting into being new conditions for living.

Shadow Mountain

The honey I stir into my tea raises eyebrows when friends see it's called Superfund honey. It comes from a beekeeper operating out of Collinsville, Oklahoma. He keeps bees at a former zinc smelter.

Oklahoma's EPA Region 6, near Collinsville, is awash in crimson clover; the roots don't absorb heavy metals, so honeybees—over one million of them—have migrated to the clover fields. A beekeeper at the former smelter has called the fields a golden place, saying wistfully, "It's remediated; it's back; it's beautiful; it's clean."

The honey echoes the smelter. When I eat it, I'm reminded of bee orchids, flowers that give the illusion of having a female bumblebee perched on their petals. If the orchid outlasts declining bee populations, it will become a bee memorial. My body performs memory, recalls my ancestors and also the places I've lived that constitute my being in a manner like genetics. I am both who and where I've come from; I echo.

The honey and smelter can be thought of as the echoes of the "chemical sublime," what scholar Nicholas Shapiro defines as "a sensuous reasoning that indicates how open our bodies are and amplifies—rather than extinguishes—the tensions, agitations, and dissident potentiality of large-scale hazards" moving into and then within us.

Ecologies of entanglement both surround and make me: the small changes passing between bodies and places, species and atmospheres, across time, collapse in the sweetness that coats my tongue or the orchid's petal that mirrors a bee; sweat or semen or breast milk; air or soil or water. The zinc smelter is demolished and lives inside my mouth.

When I absorb toxins, my body is transformed into a site of postindustrial waste; I have become this damaged ecology. The chemicals that quietly emanate in my home, the foods I eat, the air I breathe, the water I drink, becomes me. I breath out, reproduce, and seep the world back. For Shapiro, the "chemical sublime" elevates the symptomatic—headaches, disease, my difficult pregnancy—into "events that stir ethical consideration and potential intervention." Even in their abstract occurrence, the point to linger on isn't proof; it is potentiality. The body is in a sublime entanglement with the natural world. The chemical sublime is thrilling, terrifying, unifying—it stitches bodies to places in strange, enchanting ways. I suck my spoon or my lover's body and take in the sweetness of this place.

I recall a line from an Éireann Lorsung poem:

not *"the body"* indefinite
and general but *my own, your own.*

Not *"the body"* indefinite but maybe neither my own. Maybe this body with you, here.

I eat the honey the couple who lives next door bottles, too, from the bees they keep out back by the alley. When I eat the honey they bottle I think how we are, all of us, precise ecologies. I eat honey, and become more this block, drenched in dusk light. I eat honey and wonder at the mysterious lesions on my brain and what particulate made them and where. Was it a gradual violence? A winter, a summer, or many? Air or water or soil? I eat and wonder at my father's seeping stomach. My son's spongy young lungs. How sublime our bodies are, how sublime faces when grinning. I want to watch everyone throw their chins back and send their necks long, laughing. I think how stunning my dead were, laughing, how good it feels to be a body tangled in another's breath-on-a-bare-neck embrace, and recall a note I keep taped above my desk: "Our continued survival demands that we learn something about how best to live and die within the entanglements we have. We need both senses of monstrosity: entanglement as life and as danger."

Now it is dusk and the sun drops low over the pollinators, sending a wet gold light down the block, coating everything.

Property Relations

One day, house cleaning, I find a silver pendant in a built-in cabinet, stuck between boards from a long time ago.

On the pendant is Saint Germaine Cousin, French saint born in 1579. Her patronage: abandoned people, abuse victims, those experiencing illness and impoverishment, the loss of parents, sick people. I read on the internet all about Germaine: "From her birth she seemed marked out for suffering; she came into the world with a deformed hand and the disease of scrofula." Her father's second wife "treated Germaine with much cruelty."

I lift Germaine from the warped folds of the old pantry. The cabinet I find her in is coated in a thick yellow tobacco film. All day, I clean and paint it with pungent Kilz Hide-All.

Between the white paint and Germaine, I feel disgust at the settler archetype I embody and the long history of performances of white violence disguised as property relations, property improvements. There are no longer the same racist covenants mediating who can hold the deed to this square of unceded Dakota land and the house I live in on top of it, but I know: "Our lives are shaped by empire / our lives shape the land." I'm a ventriloquist's dummy and what I perform here is amnesia. Painting the pantry cabinet white, painting over history. Bertolt Brecht: "Those who are against Fascism without being against capitalism, who lament over the barbarism that comes out of barbarism, are like people who wish to eat their veal without slaughtering the calf. They are willing to eat the calf, but they dislike the sight of blood."

I have a responsibility to reckon with this property, on this land. My complicity in the violence of history, and the ugliness of gentrification I signify. All my body is, and all it suggests.

Mary Siisip Geniusz, in her book of Anishinaabe botanical teachings, has been teaching me, as a non-Native gardener, how the effects of colonization mediate what I see and what I fail to when I look at, for instance, mullein. There is so much I have to learn and unlearn.

Like how jewelweed survives because it self-seeds. When touched, rubbed, the plant's bean-like pods burst, reseeding the soil. Poison ivy often grows next to jewelweed, which is also called touch-me-not. The poison ivy oil gives the rash. Jewelweed sap is the balm for this, crushed stems relieving the itch. Touch-me-not needs touch, the brush of a deer's body or the light sweep of a bird's wings, to self-seed.

Or how a plant that grows back first near pollution is especially good at helping people breathe better. As an inhalant, Geniusz writes, mullein will treat asthma, and its oil cures internal bleeding.

Mullein thrives on newly turned soil, so it is one of the first plants to regrow after a woodland has been clear-cut or a highway knifed through a poor neighborhood. Mullein has long been misunderstood by European botanists: in ancient England, the dried stalks dipped in tallow to make candles were met with suspicion by the church and thought to light the way to witches' orgies.

I recall what my friend Kate said about what cocktail ants do. How they burrow into acacia thorn trees and create galls that could destroy the tree, but the tree feeds them nectar through those galls and the ant, in turn, protects the tree against herbivores. Humans could be in a different relationship with our ecosystems and each other if we better understood how symbiosis and mutual aid are the biosphere's default modes of operation.

I crack windows, the house smelling like poison, and go outside, where a breeze pushes past from the direction of Shoreham Yards. The rail yard croons. All along the sidewalk there are crooked bushy shoots of gray-green mullein.

Mullein is abundant in these streets because it heals.

Wasteland

U.S.-hospital cancer care requires considerable amounts of energy; the pharmaceutical industry is 50 percent more carbon intensive than the automotive industry; once a person has died and if they are cremated, this process creates air pollution harmful to the environment. The by-products of burning a life include fine soot, carbon monoxide, sulfur dioxide. Mercury from dental fillings.

My friend Molly took his bloody teeth in the ziplock bag away. The ones knocked loose when he fell because he was weak and had stood too soon and fainted. He broke his nose on the tiled kitchen floor, shattered the architecture of his wide mouth. It was the day after his birthday; the day before, I'd sat with him while he took small sips of a smoothie and we watched bad TV together. "I can't keep them," I said. I couldn't throw them away. We stood in my living room hours after the funeral. I was wearing a black dress, tall heels. My lips perfectly red.

All day, I would slip into the bathroom to check my mouth, at the service, the bar after. I knew how to make my body a tightly sealed receptacle, how to bury. Family complimented my appearance. I felt like a volcano. "I'll take the teeth." Molly reached for my hand.

I don't know where his teeth went next; I never asked her. I wonder if she put them in the bin on the boulevard and then they were taken by a truck to a landfill, buried under more garbage. Were they eventually incinerated, like the rest of his body but later?

Once my father became someone transformed and once I was a part of transforming him, into ash, into pollution, into bagged teeth sent away, the world of what was out of sight would not stay gone. What I buried at the bar behind my red polite mouth was in me, shifting, seething. I had the thought that what a culture or a daughter wants gone—to ignore it or to overcome it, so grief might be mastered like a carpenter would a craft—all that turned like shards of glass in a patch of soil, cutting. What I buried wasn't gone.

Molly moved toward me, pressed my palm wide. I smelled her grapefruit perfume. She took his teeth. I did not cry. I was a good vessel. Here was the weight of the blood that made me, and she held it. His teeth looked like young watermelon seeds. We also bury seeds, I realized, we plant our dead and our desire for more life in the same earth. The blood at the base of the translucent bag gathered like flecks of loose soil.

Roads to Take

"These are roads to take when you think of your country," writes Muriel Rukeyser about her drive from New York City to central Appalachia in 1936. She repeats this line throughout *The Book of the Dead*, the documentary poems she created in response to the industrial tragedy at Hawk's Nest.

In Hawk's Nest, migrant laborers, most of whom were Black men up from the South seeking work during the Depression, were sickened with silicosis, a known disease. Tunneling released silica dust into the air; a white powder that scars lungs and killed an estimated 764 men by acute silicosis and others years and decades later. The corporation denied blame and set lawyers to the task of obfuscating the links between illness and silica dust. Rukeyser's writing of witness would get her on the FBI's watchlist.

Driving through Picher, Oklahoma, with my boyfriend, heading to Tulsa, we pass a strange sight—windowless abandoned houses made from uniformed red brick, spray-painted with the words *keep out*. Pale hills swell the distance.

Later I'll learn we were passing through the heart of the Tar Creek Superfund, a tristate, forty-seven-square-mile area that human-created environmental catastrophes have left uninhabitable and emptied of people; like Pripyat, Ukraine, after the nuclear disaster at the Chernobyl nuclear-plant reactor; or Centralia, Pennsylvania, where an underground coal mine has been burning since 1962 and spreading through tunnels and is predicted to smolder for another two hundred years.

In Picher, contamination from lead and zinc pit mines extending hundreds of feet under homes, and from unearthed chat hills, grainy mounds pregnant with lead, zinc, and cadmium, shuttered the town. In 1983, Picher was declared the heart of contaminated prairieland spanning Oklahoma, Kansas, and Missouri, and the sovereign lands of nine tribal nations—the Quapaw, Seneca-Cayuga, Miami, Modoc, Wyandotte, Ottawa, Peoria, Eastern Shawnee, and Cherokee.

At the turn of the twentieth century, found to be mineral-rich, this swath of prairie was force-leased by the U.S. government and sold to private mining companies. Throughout the 1890s, Quapaw tribal members who did not want to sign unfavorable leases were labeled "incompetent" in federal documents. Under the violent logic of white supremacy, backed by political theft, billions of dollars of minerals were unearthed. Quapaw landowners rarely received lease payments or mined-mineral royalties.

In Hawk's Nest, the Union Carbide and Carbon Corporation is at work constructing a three-mile tunnel in 1930, to divert water from the New River to a plant downstream, to generate power for iron smelting. Workers dry-blasted the mountain for eighteen straight months. Silica dust powdered the men in mineral shards, fine as glass, that lodged into the pink of their lungs.

During Picher's boom, there were 14,252 residents living in pastel clapboard homes nestled among white hills that look like the gypsum crystal sand dunes in White Sands, New Mexico. The mined lead and zinc was melted into bullets fired during both world wars. The Tri-State Mining District, now the Tar Creek Superfund, thrived economically out of a condition of war.

In 2008, a devastating F4 tornado toppled most of the buildings left in Picher, leveling physical markers of the mining town's past. The chat hills remain, and so do the health problems people face that stretch over decades and move between generations and present a difficult-to-categorize trauma.

How are such losses as these remembered and told? Who should speak for the dead? Picher was not my disaster, neither was Hawk's Nest for Rukeyser, but maybe they belong to a menagerie of losses caused by industrial extraction and removal—of minerals, and of lives.

There are hardly any markers in Hawk's Nest to memorialize the disaster, the many men who died and were buried in unmarked graves. This is not oversight, but racist redaction in a state that celebrates miners' legacies yet attempted to cover up a horrific event, to strike it from public memory. Photographer Raymond Thompson, Jr., in his series Appalachian Ghosts, uses archival images to develop life-sized portraits of the Black men who tunneled the dam. His work seeks to remember, to "feel their presence," to correct corporate and government erasure and honor "the history of those left behind," countering "historical amnesia."

These are roads to take. Flooded with memory and loss.

In Picher, I sight a bit of floral dinner dish in tall grasses and remember sorting my father's things in the days after he died. How the room smelled like him. What generous haunting. The apartment, briefly, alive.

One night in Tulsa I open Rukeyser's book and read:

Do they seem to fear death? . . .

They want to live as long as they can.

Roadside utility pole and chat pile in Picher, Oklahoma.

Floodwaters

Months after the rains arrived in Tulsa, after the flash flooding and tornadoes, the night we slept in the basement of my love's apartment building and woke to a cloudless city lit sharp as a blue glass bowl, I wanted to go swimming, so Moheb took me to Skiatook Lake. The lake is a reservoir in Osage County, Oklahoma, within the boundaries of the Osage Nation, the Indigenous tribe of the Great Plains the county is named for and home to, twenty-five miles northwest of Tulsa.

At Skiatook, I felt self-conscious in my bathing suit, too naked, too soft. Moheb urged me to swim, to ignore the No Swimming sign posted to the dock we'd claimed after a family of women and dogs moved down shore to splash in an empty boat ramp. It was one hundred degrees. A white plastic bag floated by us on the surface of the water. I dipped my toes in. He closed his eyes next to me. The family down shore was playing a game called dead man. *Dead man, dead man, come alive!* The sounds of laughter, their dogs barking.

After the floods, an eight-year-old with chronic kidney disease was rushed to Oklahoma Children's Hospital, where he remained for nearly three weeks. He had been exposed to E. coli while swimming in Bluestem, another Osage County lake. Floodwaters have contaminated lakes throughout the state, including Skiatook, and Payne County residents with an open cut touched by floodwaters have been urged by the Federal Emergency Management Agency to get a tetanus booster immediately. We ignore the warnings and swim.

I eased my body off the dock, ducked my head underwater. The matter of what water my body gets I mostly can't choose. A small thrill, then, to be aware of the potential dangers. Briefly, to be choosing them.

Oklahoma is full of pit lakes. After a mining operation moves out, the pit fills with aquifer water that seeps in.

The water was warm as a heated pool but I felt good in it, moving my concealed body, gummy and loose.

"When can we go dancing?" my father had asked, still high, after his last stomach cancer operation.

I was swimming and then he came to mind, in the ICU, hooked up to machines, all those months ago. I wondered about everyone he thought he was seeing waking up those long days in the ER. My mother? A lover? He knew he loved dancing. He knew dancing was better with two bodies.

The lake is the municipal water supply for the cities of Skiatook, Sand Springs, Sapulpa, and Tulsa. Surrounded by tallgrass prairie and knotty post oaks, constructed by the Flood Control Act in 1962, this was the water we'd go home to Moheb's apartment and drink tonight, treated first, and the result of a dammed pit mine.

Driving home through alfalfa fields, we watched cows graze amid petroleum pipelines, pump jacks bending in a slow rhythm. We passed the prison, passed the dairy distributor. After sundown, in a Dollar General parking lot, we shared a warm beer.

Technically speaking, my father died by drowning. Pneumonia that came on quick. His lungs filled with water that seeped, pooled, and could not be contained.

The Zone

A toxin threatens, but it also beckons.

—Mel Y. Chen

Andrei Tarkovsky's film *Stalker* isn't about stalking or gender violence but the strange enchantment cast by a deeply polluted environment. It opens with the lines, "Whatever it was, in our small country,
there appeared a miracle—the Zone. We sent in troops. Not one
returned. Then we surrounded the Zone with a security cordon."

In newspaper interviews with EPA-evacuated residents from various
cities, many people don't believe this is happening where they live:
lead poisoning, cancers, water pollution; corporate and government
cover-ups; necessary evacuations. Simultaneously, such accounts tell
of people who are growing in their understanding that they take these
places with them, inside their cells. As Rob Nixon has observed in his
book *Slow Violence and the Environmentalism of the Poor,* "Chemical
and radiological violence, for example, is driven inward, somatized
into cellular dramas of mutation that—particularly in the bodies of
the poor—remain largely unobserved, undiagnosed, and untreated."

"Think about your daughter," Stalker's wife beseeches at the beginning of Tarkovsky's film. Stalker is leaving again. He's leaving his
family for the Zone.

The movie is a masculine journey story. Three men go to the Zone for absurd yet deeply felt personal reasons. There's Stalker, Writer, and Professor, a physicist.

"What's in the Zone for you?" the men ask each other in a bar, getting drunk together. Professor feels called to it. Writer is going for inspiration. He wants to take some of the rumored power of the place, use it for his own gain. There's a place in the Zone where desires come true.

When I go, I fear I'm perpetuating the extractive. *What's in it for me?* Tarkovsky, in an interview, said: "To tell of what is living, the artist uses something dead; to speak of the infinite, he shows the finite." Days, I walk the fences, lugging my grief. On-screen, the men drive through sepia-hued industrial wastelands that are heavily patrolled. They duck a patrolman who fires at them.

When I'd visit Oklahoma, I started driving to the Tar Creek Superfund alone. I didn't expect to meet anyone; it had been described as a ghost town. A few times, I was stopped by state troopers. They asked why I had come. There was concern, a talkative young deputy marshal told me one afternoon, that I was an illegal poacher. Out-of-state plates, like mine, usually meant deer poaching.

"You're just a conceptual poacher," Moheb teased, kissing my cheek later that night back in the Tulsa apartment.

What does my curiosity about these violated places play out, exactly? On-screen, Writer is absorbed in a monologue of self-loathing: "What I said about going there it's all a lie. I don't give a damn about inspiration. But how can I put a name to what it is that I want?" Tipped-over oil drums in stagnant water. Bits of scrap metal. The men drive through piles of piping, stacked lumber.

I tear up when the sepia disappears suddenly and is replaced by green trees and blue skies, utility poles, a rusted car in tallgrass prairie. Stalker says, "Here we are, home at last." They've reached the Zone.

The foggy ruin on-screen is familiar. In my childhood backyard, we kept stacked lumber, building materials. I don't wish to fetishize ruin or add to the exoticizing of such landscapes, but how do I reconcile that postindustrial, often-polluted places contain for me a comfort? A feeling of being home, at last.

"It's so still," Stalker says, his voice shaking. "It's the quietest place on earth. You'll see for yourself. It's so beautiful. There's no one here."

It occurs to me, watching, that a part of me loves the Zone, and that there is a violence that lives in this affection. In the film, Stalker's daughter is described as "a mutant," a so-called Zone victim.

In a fight between the men, Stalker walks away from them and shouts over his shoulder: "The Zone is a very complex maze of traps. All of them are death traps. I don't know what happens here when humans aren't around. But as soon as humans appear, everything begins to change."

His paranoia recalls other European and American pollution-driven environmental art and theorizing that emerged during the 1960s and '70s, the film's cultural moment, that also conveyed a paternalistic ecological mistrust. In social scientist Gregory Bateson's 1972 book, *Steps to an Ecology of Mind,* human health and natural and cultural environments were seen as linked by way of an abusive relationship. Humans have taken liberties; the natural world will now attack humanity back. Bateson writes: "In the present instance, we begin to know some of Nature's ways of correcting the imbalance—smog, pollution, DDT poisoning, industrial wastes, famine, atomic fall-out, and war. *But the imbalance has gone so far that we cannot trust Nature not to over-correct* [Bateson's italics]."

Is nature the "stalker" the three men fear? This imaginary erases the perpetrators and specific culpability for colonial and extractive violence and invites a larger critique of sixties and seventies environmental and land art, which is the movement's nostalgia and desire to return to the precolonial through new land management. On-screen, the same white masculine delusions play out; the marginalized and abused are to be feared by those with power because one day the oppressed will rise up and burn existing power structures to the ground. Let this be true.

Leaving Picher one day, I spot a barn owl on a tall tree branch. The owl's plumage is thick and gorgeous against the pale blue sky threaded with jet contrails. It is possible to imagine this place evolving a kind of ecological balance, now that the miners who abused it are gone.

The Zone is lush. Stalker falls to his knees surrounded by tall grasses and inhales deeply. He plants his face in the soil, and an insect crawls over his knuckles slowly. He rolls in the green until his clothes glisten with dew.

The film was shot in Estonia near the capital of Tallinn in the summer of 1977. Parts of the film were shot in a disused refinery. The crew stood in puddles of oil and the effluent waste from an upriver paper-processing plant for hours on end as they shot.

I had sensationalized Superfunds before I understood them to be, like the Zone, gorgeous, lush, familiar places that don't visibly broadcast the threats they pose. Places that attract insects and animals.

"Be careful when you walk here," Stalker warns. Stalker feels both terror and reverence for the Zone.

In a final scene, Professor has made a bomb. "Obviously there must be a principle—never to perform irreversible actions," he says. He wants to destroy the Zone for all its ambiguity and threat and promise for wish fulfillment. Professor doesn't understand what seems obvious: his destructive solution will feed the Zone.

Stalker is in tears at the sight of the bomb. He asks the men not to deprive him of what's his, the Zone. He says, "Everything I have is here."

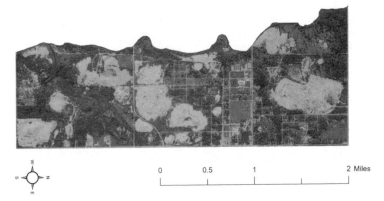

Tar Creek and chat piles in Picher, Oklahoma. The curved edge is the movement of the creek.

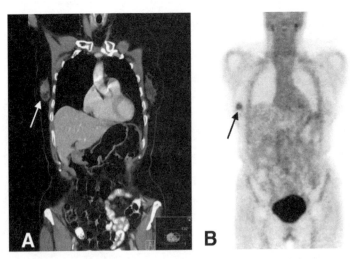

CT reconstruction (a) and PET scan (b) of 69-year-old patient with invasive ductal carcinoma.

Chat Piles

Windy July day, over one hundred degrees in Picher. Chat piles—bright silt bluffs carved and shaped by wind and rain and tornados and cut by ATV tire and animal tracks—interrupt the flat horizon. When fine particles of chat dust catch the air, my clothes and skin go chalky. Picher chat contains toxic metals, siliceous rock, limestone, and dolomite waste.

Before Picher was evacuated and unincorporated, deemed too toxic to live in by the federal government, children took refuge from Oklahoma's pressing summer heat swimming in creeks ruddy with cadmium and arsenic. At dusk, families picnicked on chat under broad, uninterrupted sunlight. At night, teenagers grabbed at each other's bodies on hills bright as moonscape, faintly glowing.

Today, at the base of a chat hill, I see a metal desk chair pointed toward the chat, deflated cardboard box of beer beside it. Maybe the chair was blown over during the last tornado to devastate Picher, the F4 moving at a wind speed of two hundred miles per hour. Or it was carried away from an abandoned building by someone some sunset. Beer from a nearby Miami, Oklahoma, gas station, bought after a shift at Teeter's Asphalt and Materials.

I walk up to the chair, sit down, and stare at the rising hill until my eyes sting from the blowing dust and I look away, in the direction of Lytle Creek. Past cracked roadways barely getting traffic and busted mine shafts, more pale swells rise in the near distance. I am alone. I am someone's mother and someone's daughter. My eyes, mouth. A chalky dust, the taste of it. How easily my body opens.

Downstream

On a dense winter night in Minneapolis, St. Anthony Falls is lit up. My fingers burn inside my gloves from the sting of cold. I have come to the dam lock at night to see a light projection, an art installation.

I learn at the dam lock, and through artist Moira Villiard's work projected here, that Dakota women would seek the falls out as a place to give birth to the next generation. In the Dakota language, Mni Sota Makoce, from which Minnesota derives its name, means water that reflects clouds.

It is a bitingly cold night. In Tulsa, during the last hot summer, the Arkansas River flooded. My friend Liz told me how sirens called an "odd birdsong" all day and night, ringing across a land of "windsweep and tornadoes."

When I was a child in Minnesota, my sight didn't reach to Oklahoma. Nowhere south, or downstream, really. Not even past the falls.

Hundreds of years ago, the Quapaw tribe moved down the Mississippi River into Arkansas. Their migration was the origin of the word Ogaxpa, which translates to "downstream people."

On weekends, when I visit Oklahoma now, I drive from Tulsa to the Tar Creek Superfund. Here, cave-ins of abandoned pit mines could be complete and sudden. Stands of full-grown cottonwoods just dropping down into the earth, still standing upright.

Picher, Oklahoma, has been sensationalized in national narratives and belongs to a constellation of ruin porn–type places. It has been described as "America's most toxic town," "abandoned," and "the biggest environmental disaster you've never heard of."

Environmental racism reaches beyond the scope of the physical and into the imaginary, as when news articles depict large sections of Ottawa County as "abandoned" or "empty."

Centuries before the Arkansas Territorial and U.S. government forcibly relocated the Quapaw Tribe from their homelands to Oklahoma, the Quapaws were a division of a larger group known as the Dhegiha Sioux. They split into the Quapaw, Osage, Ponca, Kansa, and Omaha tribes when they left the Ohio Valley. Moved down the Mississippi River and into Arkansas to where the two rivers met, the Arkansas and Mississippi. The tribe settled beside a river tributary with nutrient-rich soil, good to farm.

In 2013, when the Quapaw Tribe negotiated a remedial-response cooperative agreement with the EPA to self-perform the remediation of a historic and culturally significant tribal property called the Catholic 40, they spearheaded, in Tar Creek, the first-ever Tribal-led Superfund cleanup in the nation.

In Tar Creek, Indigenous community leaders are protecting and remediating their land and water. The Quapaw tribe is the first tribal nation funded by the EPA in their remediation and reclamation work.

The Tar Creek Superfund, the land and water and air damaged by white violence, is being remediated by Indigenous leaders now. So it is a further violence for such a place to be thought of as a "ghost town" or "empty" or "creepy," though a quick online search confirms the dominance of this narrative in online culture's imaginary.

At the dam, in Minnesota, I stand on the unceded lands of the Dakota. A deed affirms that a square of this unceded land is now legally "mine." This deed is evidence not of ownership but of complicity. It affirms a legacy violence that I am a part of, that I uphold by my presence here. How to reckon with this? How to heal it? What to do with my one life now, next, here?

It is important to allow for the incommensurability of difference, Max Liboiron observes in their book *Pollution Is Colonialism*. "Indigenous peoples, settlers, and others have different roles and responsibilities in the challenge to invent, revive, and sustain decolonizing possibilities and persistences."

How might I live in greater allegiances with Indigenous communities, I wonder, and with this land, without glossing over my own guilt, and my responsibilities? Liboiron: "You can't have obligation without specificity." And there is no room for "we." Who floods? Not we, but maybe you do / I do.

Moira Villiard projects blue and red light onto the concrete walls of the dam. In an essay accompanying her installation, Suenary Philavanh asks a question about resilience: "Resilience: for a Native woman living in an urban, concrete jungle, what does that look like?"

From Tulsa, Liz writes of the flood and all that it wears down, "You, earth-carved scar, swollen artery, / keep coming."

Liboiron references anthropologist Kim TallBear's methodological approach of "standing with" and "inquiring among" as well as Michelle Murphy's scholarship on alterlife: "Political kinship . . . comes out of the recognition of connected, though profoundly uneven and often complicit, imbrications in the systems that distribute violence." I think of living downstream. How Quapaw harks to an older history than polluted waterways and land in Oklahoma and the remediation work that the tribe is actively carrying out there now, but widens out to reach the banks of the Mississippi. A river I was born inside a tall hospital looking out over, in a steel and concrete tower.

The Quapaw tribe migrated downriver and made a home among rich coursing water, lively soil. *Downstream,* and the relationship the tribe has to the location has nothing to do with pollution, really—the pollution they endure, now, and work to remediate.

Months after I go to see the dam lock installation, after a few email exchanges, in a house with a green roof in Miami, Oklahoma, I meet Rebecca Jim. We sit inside the LEAD Agency, standing for Local Environmental Action Demanded, in a warm house at the outskirts of downtown. This is the only environmental justice organization within Tar Creek advocating for its cleanup. We talk. I tell her about my father. She tells me it sounds as if there are similarities between our grief.

Though there are also profound differences between us. So we sit. We talk. Hours pass. Meanwhile, time laps the banks.

Superfund Cleanup didactic, EPA region 6, northeastern, Oklahoma.

From: Rebecca Jim

The Tar Creek Superfund, Oklahoma

I live on the Cherokee Reservation, twenty-five miles away from where I work. I live on a tallgrass prairie that I'm restoring. It's got some invasive species that I'm working on removing by burning the fields, like the old ways. I built my house. My dad and I checked out books from the library and built it together. I centered it near the creek that runs below it. So I can go down to water, as a Cherokee should, every day, go to clean water. But when I leave here and go to my work, the water is not clean, and so there's some deep regret that there are people in that community where I work and people around the country, around the world, who cannot take water for granted and cannot use what they've got.

I went to work in Miami, Oklahoma, as the school's Indian counselor. I worked there twenty-five years in the secondary junior high and with high-school-age youth. I started this work the year before Tar Creek turned orange, and it is still orange. It's still running heavy metal, a million gallons every day for over fifteen thousand days.

I started working in that school district in '78, but it wasn't until '93 that we understood that so many of our Indian kids were lead poisoned, and that lead poisoning could affect the way they learn, the way they react, their social decisions, could easily cause attention deficit disorder or for them to be hyperactive. Once that was discovered and reported to the EPA, the EPA had to react.

So we were on the first list that the EPA established, the Superfund's National Priorities List. We were listed number one in the nation. They filled some mine shafts and closed some wells, trying to lessen the amount of water that went back into the aquifer. They took some actions, but they weren't very effective.

Then Lois Gibbs went on TV on the morning program. She took children and went on the morning shows. They had posters with hand-drawn hearts all over, and here are these children, and she's saying this place, Love Canal, is damaged and children are being harmed and EPA should do something about it. And Superfund left us, really, and went to Love Canal.

It was only the fact that it became known that our children were lead poisoned that made the EPA eventually come back. They came back and have spent over $400 million here. They've still not done anything to improve the water at Tar Creek, or the fact that when it floods it spreads its toxins in yards, playgrounds, any other place, fields where crops are grown. And then eventually it flows

into the Grand Lake o' the Cherokees, which is the water I drink
out of my faucet.

I'm the Tar Creekkeeper. I'm the water protector. It doesn't matter
which water it is, I'm going to work for it to run clean and be able
to generate the kind of life that any species might need to exist
there. Tar Creek doesn't have many species of fish, and that's really
not right. But it can be repaired—it's not nuclear waste. This is
fixable. This is something that communities around the world have
been able to deal with, restoring damaged water like this. I'm saying, it's not a pipe dream, it's a real possibility, and I'm going to ride
that pony and try to make it happen.

Why are we sick with this, how come? That was a question that kept
coming up. Questions about health kept coming up. The very sad
light bulbs would turn on when I begin to think: *That's what's killing my friend.* But we can't get a cancer-cluster designation because
there's not enough dead here yet. You've got to have a lot of dead
people to qualify for cancer clusters. Very often, there's not enough.
There was a moment in time when EPA started figuring out how
they could match like communities, those communities that had the
same kinds of exposures, and add them up so that yes, *now* there's a
cluster. A cluster could be in five different places, but it would still be
a cancer cluster. That was so powerful, because then communities

could make the case that a particular chemical or set of chemicals in their area was harming them, but then that EPA effort stopped.

Things come and go with administrations and with—anyway, it's those light bulbs that go on when someone has either buried a husband, a wife, and then they get activated to do a thing, and then sometimes they die too. I have buried my best activist, and some of my students too. I'm twice as old as they are, and they're dying or they're on kidney dialysis. So it drives me to keep working on their behalf and to keep speaking out and hollering on behalf of this water, this place.

My son has asthma, like you. I've wondered that myself, *How did that happen?* Did I take him to work with me too much when he was young? Did I expose him at the times when he was most vulnerable? I think any mother wonders, *How did that happen? What am I doing wrong? Am I not a good enough house cleaner? Did I give this to my baby?* There's a lot of guilt and a lot of shame that living near a toxic site can cause.

Tar Creek flows through the middle of the country, the Great Plains, the Ozark lift. The edge of Oklahoma has a bit of Ozark mountains in it. They're not really mountains, but there's an uplift, so the uplift is the boundary on the northeast part of Oklahoma, and the other boundary is the Spring River that comes through

Kansas and Missouri before it gets to us, water traveling through four other Superfund sites contaminated with lead and zinc before reaching our site, within the boundaries of Tar Creek, where the waters join up and flow south together.

We've got the uplift on one side of the river, and on the other side, the plains. The rolling plains—flat, lots of horizon, lots of sky. We have a lot of sky and we don't have a lot of people. This county was a dumping ground for nine other tribes who got stacked up here as if you put the biggest plate on top of a smaller plate. This is the last place on earth the tribes wanted to come but it was the last piece of ground they were given by the US government as they were leaving their homelands from other parts of the country and being forced out of their original homes.

We've got the Quapaw and Miami and the Peoria, we're all stacked up here. They're the tribes that had ore found underground on their lands. Then below them are the other tribes. Wedged between those tribes and the Spring River is the Grand River. Where the Neosho and the Spring River meet they form the Grand River. The Grand River is dammed, and the first dam forms the Grand Lake o' the Cherokees.

This land was tallgrass prairie. It was a hay capital of the country. Tall hay, rich for cattle. The cattle are what brought some of the white settlers in, ranchers, to raise cattle in this area, and in order to stay and not have to lease the land, many of them, like my grandfather, found him a good Cherokee woman to marry so he could raise cattle without paying any lease money.

This land up here, we were rich in grass, but the upper portions of Ottawa County, they were rich in ore. Beneath their ground was a vast amount of lead and zinc. And digging it out of the ground, the miners burrowed down and made shafts into it because it's not open pit digging. They dug down below and made a room, hollowed out a room and got the ore out and then hollowed out another room. Miners did that across forty square miles where the ore was found. They dug into an aquifer, and in order to do it, they pumped it dry for sixty years. And when they abandoned the site they turned off the pumps and the aquifer refilled. All of those metals were still exposed, and so they brewed in there like a toxic tea, and that's what spews out still.

There's no tallgrass prairie up there now. That's been replaced by white mountains of mine waste, chat. They look like sand dunes in Colorado and Texas and New Mexico.

My mother, who died at the age of ninety-two, she slid down those mountains when she was a teenager. She slid down those piles for fun, because it was. Many generations used those piles as recreation, not knowing that every time they took their socks off back at home they were also bringing a load of heavy metals inside with them. This stuff blows in the wind, and then it was later hauled all over the county to make driveways and alleys, to be put under swing sets in front yards and backyards and playgrounds and schoolyards. It's been distributed, that waste, that poison, to neighborhoods and children, for the next generation.

We've got chat piles that are coming down because they're being sold. That's what the Quapaw are doing right now, they're taking down their chat piles and selling them. That waste is going to other communities. The last batch, I think it's going to Puerto Rico. It's supposed to be used in safe manners, in roadbeds or as asphalt, but roadways have to be remade and roadways are redone by neighborhoods, so I think it's true that what poisoned us can poison others.

That's the work they're doing right now, to remediate. Getting down to pastures to make them into hay meadows, crop fields. The Quapaw are also leaving some of this waste behind that they can't sell. Those are going to look like Cahokia Mounds. They're going to look like the mounds that many of our tribal nations are related to and built. Some chat piles will be left as structures, monuments to a hard past. I think we'll remember them that way.

When I was driven, like so many other water protectors, to head out to Standing Rock, I took my son and we went up. We were there when Obama refused to allow it.

When we went up, crossing the Missouri River, every time we crossed that river I rolled down the window because you can smell the fresh water. We don't have the beautiful freshwater smell here in Oklahoma. We don't have that, it doesn't smell like that, but it was there because that water hasn't been damaged. Not polluted, tainted, but cared for. Anyway, we were there when all that happened, and we got to see the fireworks go off just as the blizzard was coming on. We left as the blizzard came down on the highway. Driving through all that snow, and all you can get out that way is country music, and we turned on the radio and it was that song, "A Thousand Miles from Nowhere," and we were, we really were.

Tar Creek

Clouds rise over the turnpike in shifting blocks of light, pale to bruise, and in the near distance lightning flares. I'm past Catoosa with its roadside blue-whale attraction, a relic of old Route 66, and up through Claremore and Vinita by the time the sky cracks a clap of thunder and lets loose rain while I greet Rebecca Jim in the front yard of her nonprofit in Miami, Oklahoma.

The rain moves us inside the LEAD Agency, headquartered since 1997 in a single-family house with yolk-yellow walls. We've made plans to go to Tar Creek today. Inside, we wait out the rain with Rebecca's son, Dana, a civil rights attorney and formerly the assistant attorney general for the Cherokee Nation, who is wearing a T-shirt that reads: "I flood and I vote." In 2019, regions of eastern Oklahoma, including Miami, flooded, and the LEAD Agency and Waterkeeper Alliance took aerial footage and documented the flooded wastewater treatment plants, three coal-fired power plants, farmlands, the Tar Creek Superfund site, cities, and the waters of the Grand Lake, which supplies drinking water to the region. When the creek floods, it washes the deposition and sedimentation of toxic heavy metals into the yards of homes and public areas. In some yards, the soil has already been remediated by the EPA. "Will EPA have to come back sometime and clean all this soil up again?"

Rebecca asked in a piece on the flooding published by *Oklahoma Energy Today.*

Rebecca hands me a cold Coca-Cola. Dana has been helping her repair the free library box in the front yard when I arrive, and while we catch up inside, he runs to the hardware store for more wood caulk. We wait out the storm. The last time we met was in this house, years ago. We'd made plans to get together more frequently in the intervening years, whenever I was visiting Tulsa, but when the world shuttered as the pandemic raged we spoke on the phone instead, about the river and my father's death and the pollution in her neighborhood and mine. I feel a sense of reunion in the calm dense rooms of her agency, among stacks of books, file folders containing fish consumption and mercury study results; voting paperwork from a campaign she recently carried out advocating for Tar Creek. Window ledges hold water samples. Framed watercolor paintings of the creek line the walls. There's a certificate of participation from the fifth-annual Picher-Cardin "coming home for Christmas" parade, a holiday memorial to the former town. Hanging over the doorframe leading from the back offices to the kitchen is a giant cardboard check presented to LEAD by the Superfund National Bank, Dallas, Texas, in the amount of $50,000.

"We didn't win our campaign," Rebecca tells me, "but it was a success anyway because so many people signed our petition. So many people showed up and cared about the creek." Our mouths are covered by masks, but her eyes show her smile.

When the sky clears and after Dana returns from the hardware store, we all go to the creek together. I follow them in my car. We park behind a nursing home under a shade tree and walk a short distance down to the water.

I'm not sensitive to the creek's daily rhythms like Rebecca, but I notice a stillness. She assesses the water. "Look," she says, addressing Dana and pointing downstream. "It's been dammed." We walk down the shores along a vegetated path to a makeshift line of concrete block and bricks zigzagging the water. "This wasn't here before," she says to Dana. "Was it?" "No way," he replies.

There are two dams. The water stilled to make a fishing hole. Though the creek is one of the most toxic waterways in the U.S., there are no signs along its banks warning anyone. The water is lined with homes, and backyards give way to it. When I comment on the lack of posted signs—nothing noting the well-documented health risks posed by exposure to the water—Rebecca chuckles.

"What an idea, signs! We put them up but then people take them down."

It's only eight miles upstream from where we stand to Douthat, where the land around the creek swells with chat piles and the water is fenced and lined with No Trespassing signs. We are downstream. For an outsider to this stretch of creek, it would be impossible to know what's upstream from where we stand, or to imagine it.

Then Rebecca is knee-deep in the creek pulling at the hunks of cement that stop the water. "This damming is a violation of her right to flow," she says. Dana follows her in. I wade in next.

"Kids aren't going to like that you're doing that," a man's voice calls down from the banks. He's riding a cherry-red dirt bike and has hit the breaks to watch us. "They dam it up to fish it," he says.

"It's not safe to do that," Rebecca replies, unphased, continuing to pull at the concrete hunks. "You want to come down here and help us free this water?" The man sits on his bike, assessing us. His bike gleams. It's Saturday, late afternoon after a storm. The sky is gray and gentle. "I tell those kids, *Don't drink it.* I know it's not safe to drink. But they swim in it. They jump in the creek off of that tree over there." The man points downstream. "They're not going to like that it's not dammed up anymore. They worked hard at it all summer long."

I follow Rebecca and Dana's lead. We pull at the hunks of cement. The dam has stopped scraps of rusting metal and pooled a pair of boxer briefs stained orange; a syringe. We pull at the concrete and the water flows harder. The man on his dirt bike has walked down to the banks. He leans on a tree trunk beside us.

Then he gets to talking. He's telling us that he's the grandson of miners. He wants to talk about how the lead came from a meteor billions of years ago that landed in present-day Missouri. He's read a geological survey of Tar Creek someone posted on Facebook, and what happened here—with the pollution and lead poisoning and everything—if you really think about it, ties this place to the cosmos. He fans his hand as if spanning a lit up marquee when he gets to the word *cosmos*. He and Rebecca know some of the same people in town; this one mutual acquaintance just bought a chat pile near Picher. The water now moving drowns out his voice. I hear bits and pieces. He's hoping his buddy, who he calls a slumlord, doesn't use that pile for illegal dumping. "Of what?" I ask. "Oh, he's got this trailer park in Tulsa near the fairgrounds, so he might just pile on that chat moldy building materials and whatever other crap he wants." "I thought the Quapaw Tribe owned all the chat over there," I say. He and Rebecca shake their heads at me. "It's not so simple," Rebecca says. "It's all gridded up that way." Ownership of the land and the chat can be separated, I learn from them, depending on where the chat is located.

The man rides off, and I ask Rebecca how she knows him. She was a high-school guidance counselor in the area for decades, so people recognize her. "Maybe I know him; maybe I don't. It's a small town. People know each other here or at least they think they do."

"Maybe he built this dam," Dana says.

"I don't think so," Rebecca says. "But we'll never know."

After we free the concrete blocks and the water rushes harder we scale up the banks. I've got a case of warm soda waters in the trunk of my car that I retrieve and pass around. We sit on the slab of concrete the man rode away on heading toward nearby dirt-bike trails. "So," Rebecca says. We are sweaty and muddy from our work. "This is a day in the life of Tar Creek," she laughs.

"It's not usually so eventful," Dana says, sipping the soda water.

In truth, I didn't expect to feel the creek's rush and pull today. I did not imagine the kids who live near the creek. The two dams they'd turn into a makeshift pool. How inviting and benign the water looks, fun to swim; to dam and fish. The creek downstream from the Superfund outside the nearby nursing home, where two nurses laugh and smoke, their voices carrying on the breeze. And on a sweltering Oklahoma summer day, if I were a kid, I'd scale a trunk and jump in the water.

"I'm glad to be here with you today," I say. "Thank you for bringing me."

"We really helped her today," Rebecca glances at the creek. "She needed our help and we gave it."

I'm thinking about the dumping. Kids who dam the creek water. The gas I burned getting here. "I don't know how any of this is ever supposed to end," I say.

"These places can be tough and lonely," Rebecca offers. I remembered learning that in Tar Creek, as early as 1934, fish were dying in the creeks and rivers and farmers noticed that their cattle wouldn't drink the water. I remember reading about a man named George Mayer who lived in the area and whose show horses broke his heart. He'd train them outside Commerce, Oklahoma. That's where he'd break them, feed them, groom them, until their hooves stained with acid mine water, so he sold them off. He couldn't afford to follow them because no one wanted his land.

"You know, I was sitting right here when Dana freed the waters upstream. I heard the creek clear her throat. Then, the more water that was unblocked, the more noise she made. The water is more free tonight and that's how this day ends, so this is a good day," Rebecca says.

Driving back to Tulsa, I pass fields with grazing horses and slow bending pump jacks. The sun is coming down over wet gray splotches of low-slung clouds, tit-heavy with a milky heat made from air and water and light. In the mornings, and for days after, the tips of my fingers will hold the creek. Nailbeds stained orange from iron or cadmium concentrate. It looks like I've been cooking with turmeric. Soon the trace veins wash off.

Tar Creek and chat pile, Picher, Oklahoma.

Watershed

Rampike is the name for ghost trees drowned by salt water. "Trees cannot relocate," I read in a letter I pull from my mailbox one afternoon. After the water rises, along the coastlines, whole generations of trees flood to bleached stands. It is raining in Minneapolis. Mature trees canopy parked cars. They are brown and green and thick with life.

The letter is from Rebecca. She writes that Tar Creek was recently named on a list of the nation's most endangered rivers. The America's Most Endangered Rivers report is an annual call to action to save threatened waters. The most recent list at the time of this writing included the Lower Missouri River and Minnesota's Boundary Waters, threatened by sulfide ore copper mining.

It was a newsletter. In it, she told of a recent conversation she'd participated in with Women's Earth Alliance members about feminist climate action. The Indigenous women leading this work as activists, scientists, and writers, discussed their labors to nurture families and steward the earth and its precious resources, to protect the environment "for the seven generations to come." Rebecca reflected, on their time together, "But as the climate emergency intensifies, so does the burden on our world's women."

I read my name in the next paragraph. I was surprised. She shared that I was writing about the pollution impacting Tar Creek. We are connected, she observed, the people who live among toxins, because of what we've been exposed to. We are the daughters of a place.

I thought of Julietta Singh, addressing her six-year-old daughter: "Learning to mother at the end of the world is an infinite toggle between wanting to make you feel safe and needing you to know that the earth and its inhabitants are facing a catastrophic crisis."

How to nurture in the midst of such crisis? How to grieve and speak to the future? Singh wants another world. "And when I say another world, I mean this one, toppled and reborn."

Reading Rebecca's words, I reflected on our relationship. Over the years, she'd lent me books on Tar Creek; I mailed her books I thought she'd like as thanks; we shared conversations; she knew her testimony would be in the book I was writing. We developed an intimacy. Solitude can be a form of privilege, but a relationship is a mutuality and a responsibility. I was in a relationship not only with places, I understood, but also with her.

She wrote: "If you want it better, care about it, say so. Loudly. Take note of what you can do. Read and study. And then act."

I have wondered how my father would feel about this strange quest. We never discussed it. He needed to believe that he would be well, that no matter what caused it, he would overcome his disease. I have felt guilt that I needed to dig, to perform this brutal autopsy. I have no proof of the relationship between land violence and his diagnosis. One day, I read my mail and realized I had met someone I now considered to be a friend, who invited me to join her in serving the creek she fiercely protected. If my father knew that through grief, a day would come when I felt less alone in my living because of people showing care and responsibility for this damaged earth, people who trusted me to work alongside them, to topple and to birth, I think he would love knowing death had delivered me here.

Bound (i.5), 2019, Exhibition: "Beyond Measure," Tali Weinberg, Tulsa, Oklahoma.

What Is Birthed?

In Tulsa, I've come to a gallery opening on Lewis Avenue to see Tali Weinberg's weavings of extractive industry, illness, and displacement.

At the gallery, bright-hued tapestries soften the stark white room. A hose made from petrochemical-derived medical tubing spirals across a low pedestal. The tube wrapped in plant-dyed string is shaded ocher, sand brown and conifer green. Colors bleed.

My friend Liz tells me at the gallery that she thinks of Tali's work like this: A violence happens and first comes emotion but the feeling soon walks down the line of reason looking for answers. Tali's weavings reverse this order. She takes climate data from the National Oceanic and Atmospheric Administration, takes the conclusions, and abstracts the data into feeling, into grieving. The results lead to an emotional outcome. "When I look at them, I cry," Liz says. Her arm casually rests atop her stomach. She is in her third trimester of pregnancy.

Introducing her installation at the opening, Tali shared a memory of the Arkansas River from her early years in Tulsa. The river was a brown trickle rimmed by oil refineries back then, but two years later, installing this show, *Bound,* she recalled the more recent spring flood, after a month of storms that transformed the riverbank into overflowing water that swallowed up homes and unearthed plastic waste from nearby landfills. Next, Tali quoted Donna J. Haraway, from her book *Staying with the Trouble.* "How can we think in times of urgencies *without* the self-indulgent and self-fulfilling myths of apocalypse, when every fiber of our being is interlaced, even complicit, in the webs of processes that must somehow be engaged and repatterned?"

Walking the gallery, I wonder if my body will ever round with life again, like Liz's. If I will birth my complicity in all of this, against my will. And I wonder if seeing clearly the interconnection between polluted places, human and nonhuman life, and future generations can be an alternative to the separation and extraction on which ecological abuses have long been premised. Maybe this is wonder, or grief by a different name.

I stand before a weaving of watersheds. Water flows within a diffuse net of permeable vessels like the movement of fluid inside bodies. The movements of blood and milk.

I think about how legacy ecological violence and other legacies of white supremacist thought and action thrive on imagining a world of separations and hierarchies that are not actual but invented to uphold such wrongs. I am as polluted as the sites. Could there be something humbling and revolutionary in understanding myself as a site of contamination? Inheritor of my ancestors' trash and misdeeds? Could restorative action and real redress grow out of this painful recognition?

I live both up- and downstream. A didactic accompanying Tali's work poses a series of questions: "If one understands home as a watershed, rather than a city or state, can that interrupt the patriarchal, colonial thinking that divides our understanding of here and away, self and other, earth and body, nature and culture? As the detritus of our human life on land runs downstream and then circulates back through bodies, what can watersheds reveal about relationships between ecological and human health? Can the ways of water help move us past the destructive extractivism that ultimately makes us sick?"

In the gallery, I am surrounded by weavings, porous as bodies.

How?

Before hospice, questions are posed to him. *What are your main wishes? What are your main fears? Where do you want to die? How do you want to die?*

I do not ask him these questions. A social worker in the hospital room does. I sit near them while a blood-red sunset flashes out the wide window that opens onto a courtyard facing other hospital rooms, and he does not want to answer these questions, and he keeps saying back, "Whatever," and spitting into a small plastic cup, and from somewhere else I hear the words *whatever / inside us that we think needs / protection, the whatever that is / small & hasn't yet found its / way.* I've been teaching these lines to students. I've come to the hospital from class. His main wish is not to die; his main fear is to die. We do not need to speak this to know it.

How do you want to die? Whatever. *It thinks it could live / on air, on words, forever almost.* His eyes are clear and blue. Ankles hairless from chemo and smooth down to his feet. One time, he got drunk on an airplane. When the plane landed in Phoenix, he was wearing bedroom slippers and he rode the baggage claim carousel like a maniac, my aunt told me at the bar after his funeral.

A former road in the unincorporated town of Picher, Oklahoma, overgrown with trees.

Shotgun Fungi

"There is only one question:
how to love this world?"

—*Mary Oliver*

It is early fall in Minneapolis, and in the community garden plot I turn over decaying leaves and damp wood mulch. In the newly exposed corners there's a patch of shotgun fungi, clear as cooked glass noodles.

The stalks grow upright under the mulch, angling toward sunlight, each topped with a swollen bulb filled with sugar and a shiny black peridiole that looks like a poppyseed or nipple.

"What do you do when your world starts to fall apart?" Anna Lowenhaupt Tsing asks at the beginning of her book *The Mushroom at the End of the World,* a work about the matsutake mushroom, capitalist destruction, and continuing life on earth. She goes for a walk to find mushrooms.

I've been neglectful this drought summer, failing to water. Encouraging only the weeds, fungi, and soil bacteria to return. What thrives without me. Across the fence today, freight cranes shudder shipping containers down onto the steel flatbeds of trucks.

I take in this patch of shotgun fungi. Near as I understand it, the fungal body seeps onto other species. This is how tree roots and mycorrhiza fungal networks share nutrients underground. Fungi excrete digestive enzymes outside their bodies, and the enzymes can digest rocks, dead trees, and soil, breaking down nutrients and recycling them into new life. It's like they've got everted stomachs. But sometimes harmony breaks down—as when the fungus parasitizes the root, or if the plant is already full of nutrients and rejects the fungus.

I take solace in the wonder of such strange patterns and repetitions across life forms and species. The seeping stomachs of fungi and people. Fungal bodies echo what's buried, Tsing observes. Going for a walk to find mushrooms when one's world is falling apart is to go looking for "binding roots." When she finds mushrooms she knows "that there are still pleasures amidst the terrors of indeterminacy."

Here in the garden plot, the air smells like kerosene and crushed yarrow. I breathe it in and out and am stitched to this place, however imperfectly and briefly, so I bend down low and dig.

A thick heat after a rare rainfall. The VOC-monitoring well pipes glisten. Under the boulevard tree, slippery, skin-soft leaves.

Pollen-drunk bees dive back into the necks of late-season flowers for last call. A car drives by fast. Inside, someone is laughing. I have come to love this soft and violent place, where summer is ending. Where death reverberates and life returns.

NOTES

annotation as excess, leaking, gratitude

Epigraphs

Éireann Lorsung, *The Century* (Minneapolis: Milkweed Editions, 2020), 111.

Muriel Rukeyser, *The Book of the Dead* (Morgantown: West Virginia University Press, 2018), 93, 62.

Humboldt Industrial Area

City of Minneapolis, "Humboldt Industrial Park Redevelopment Plan," December 16, 2005, https://www2.minneapolismn.gov/media /content-assets/www2-documents/government/View-Humboldt -Industrial-Park-Redevelopment-Plan.pdf.

> Information about the Howe fire and other historical and contextual information is from this city report. I have relied heavily on city reports over the space of this project. They are strange. Sometimes poetic. Worthy of mistrust. In this report, for example, I learned that a creek that ran through this corporate acreage was moved sometime between 1965 and 1971, but by whom and why remains a mystery. What I don't trust in the reports is the near-universal linguistic gloss of neutrality; land reuse plans in a city with a long history of redlining and white-supremacist violence that don't discuss this history. The structural racism of legacy pollution, and the ways place is interconnected with community health, is largely absent from the reports. Instead, there's talk of redevelopment and jobs; borders are drawn; new maps made. The projected future of

land use in the area is swaddled in environmental urgency, and premised on the implicit innocence of cleanup. There is hardly ever talk of who redevelopment benefits and who it harms.

Before he illegally installed the solar panels that heat our home, they'd been used to warm a catfish farm. . . . I remember the solar panels tipped against the tall wood fence in the backyard. Our cat would lengthen his neck on them. Did they really warm our home? Maybe this detail is closer to family myth than truth. All mistakes of memory are my own.

Curtain

Plato, *The Republic,* translated by Desmond Lee (New York: Penguin Books, 1955), 147–48.

When I went to the crematorium I didn't expect to be given the choice to look. It was early morning. The sky raw with light. I drove alone. His death and my grieving were new; his funeral plans intensifying; there was much to do. Watching his body transform from flesh to ash would only happen once, here and now, and so to look at this or to look away from it was equally mired in the fraught blurriness of witness. Was watching this happen love or rubbernecking? Later, would describing this watching be spectacle or truth-telling? On that day, I felt the tension of looking completely. My decision to include this moment is a gesture of tenderness for both of us and owes much to Natalie Diaz's essay "The Quantum Theory of Suffering or Why I Look at the Moon." In it, Diaz writes: "The quantum theory of suffering is also the quantum theory of tenderness: Yes, writing about my brother is acknowledgement of his suffering, of his humanity. I am measuring his suffering on the page. I am proving my love for him. To acknowledge his existence is one type of tenderness. It is tenderness even for myself." To acknowledge the existence of us on this day is one form of tenderness, so I offer it.

Natalie Diaz, "The Quantum Theory of Suffering or Why I Look at the Moon," January 13, 2015, https://pen.org/the-quantum-theory-of-suffering-or-why-i-look-at-the-moon.

Jacques Roubaud, *Some Thing Black* (Normal, IL: Dalkey Archive Press, 1999), 73–74.

Naja Marie Aidt's writing on Roubaud's work and on "death's heavy unbearable stillness" in her memoir is stunning and was instrumental in early drafts. Roubaud and Aidt write on death and the living in lyric, moving fragments.

Naja Marie Aidt, *When Death Takes Something from You Give It Back* (Minneapolis: Coffee House Press, 2019), 25.

The Soo Line Dump

Rebecca Altman, "On What We Bury," *ISLE: Interdisciplinary Studies in Literature and Environment* 21, no. 1 (Winter 2014): 85–95, https://doi.org/10.1093/isle/isu039.

I walk the dump with Rebecca Altman's scholarship on body burden in mind. The earth is not static or fixed, Altman observes, but it "is flux and system and process . . . which means nothing stays embodied or buried forever." While not a direct quote, my inclusion of thought connected to imperfect sites of burial and the shifting activity of the earth owes much to Altman's writing and thinking throughout her essay "On What We Bury."

U.S. Department of Health and Human Services Agency for Toxic Substances and Disease Registry, "Health Consultation: Soo Line Shoreham Yard East Side," September 25, 2007, 6, https://www.atsdr.cdc.gov/hac/pha/soolineshorehamyard/soolineshorehamhc92507.pdf.

Terry Tempest Williams, *Refuge* (New York: Vintage, 1992), 219; 288–89.

> I paraphrase Terry Tempest Williams. Here's the full quote from *Refuge:* "Death is no longer what I imagined it to be. Death is earthy like birth, like sex, full of smells and sounds and bodily fluids. It is a confluence of evanescence and flesh" (219). Also from *Refuge:* "The women couldn't bear it any longer" and the reference to "the contaminated country" and the quote "We are mothers and we have come to reclaim the desert for our children" (288–89).

Shoreham Yards, Minneapolis, Minnesota, © U-Spatial.

Live Map

This piece relied on the EPA's "National Priorities List and Superfund Alternative Approach Sites" and "Superfund National Priorities List (NPL) Where You Live Map," accessed August 10, 2021, https://www.epa.gov/superfund/search-superfund-sites-where-you-live.

On Openings

Doireann Ní Ghríofa, *A Ghost in the Throat* (Windsor, Ontario: Biblioasis, 2020).

Ghríofa inspired me to imagine the maternal thefts a body performs in pregnancy. While not a direct quote, I reference *A Ghost in the Throat* when I write, "I will learn that if a woman cannot consume sufficient calcium, her body will take from her bones to give to her infant."

Here are her words that inspired mine:

"If she cannot consume sufficient calcium, for example, that mineral will rise up from deep within her bones and donate itself to her infant on her behalf, leaving her own system in deficiency. Sometimes a female body serves another by effecting a theft upon itself" (35).

Rebecca Altman, "On What We Bury," *ISLE: Interdisciplinary Studies in Literature and Environment* 21, no. 1 (Winter 2014): 85–95, https://doi.org/10.1093/isle/isu039.

My writing about body burden owes much to Altman's "On What We Bury." Here and elsewhere, I think of Altman's important contributions to this discourse. We are both mothers, and this ecological history is tied to our children's lives too. Altman: "I have passed it along against my will. Such is the legacy of our time: heavy metals, pesticides, and some classes of long-lived pollutants that did not exist when our grandmothers swam in the interior oceans of our great-grandmothers' wombs."

Anders C. Erickson and Laura Arbour, "The Shared Pathoetiological Effects of Particulate Air Pollution and the Social Environment on Fetal-Placental Development," *Journal of Environmental and Public Health,* November 26, 2014, https://www.ncbi.nlm.nih.gov/pmc/articles/PMC4276595.

I reference this article when I write about the intermediary environment between mother and fetus.

Returning

Anne Boyer, *The Undying: Pain, Vulnerability, Mortality, Medicine, Art, Time, Dreams, Data, Exhaustion, Cancer, and Care* (New York: Picador, 2020), 30, 131.

Boyer's brilliant feminist critique of biomedicine and capitalism is deeply instructive. I return to her work often.

I wish to include more of her words here to honor them: "Cancer is not a sameness eternalized in an ahistorical body, moving through a trajectory of advancing technological progress. No patient is sovereign, and every sufferer, both those marked by cancer treatment and those marked by the exhausting routine of caring for those with cancer, is also marked by our historical particulars, constellated in a set of social and economic relations" (30). Boyer, again: "The history of illness is not the history of medicine—it is the history of the world—and the history of having a body could well be the history of what is done to most of us in the interest of the few" (30).

Anna Bierbrauer, "Lost to Progress: Upper Mississippi River and Minneapolis Parks Development," *Open Rivers: Rethinking Water, Place & Community,* no. 7 (Summer 2017), https://editions.lib.umn .edu/openrivers/article/lost-to-progress.

In 1872 Horace W. S. Cleveland advocated for a Minneapolis city park system that preserved open space for public use but left this stretch of river out. . . . Historical information about the industrial stretch of the river and information on the rate of asthma-related hospitalizations relies on Bierbrauer.

On asthma, here are Bierbrauer's words that inspired mine: "Given that North Minneapolis suffers from the highest rate of asthma-related hospitalizations and the highest concentration of lead poisoning cases, these air quality issues could not be ignored. One company—a metal recycling plant was found in violation of their permit and, after a lengthy legal battle, will be moving off of the river in 2019 and has paid the City of Minneapolis $600,000 for community health programs. The soon-to-be shuttered plant is one of many contributors to poor air quality in the area, but the number of MPCA-monitored sites along the river in North Minneapolis places a large burden on nearby residences."

Bierbrauer importantly observes that it is the Upper River communities of today who are driving restoration conversations. Community members who "have historically been underserved, underrepresented, and denied riverfront access making conversations about equity, environmental justice, and transparency crucial and critical planning topics."

EPA, "OLEM Programs Address Contamination at Superfund, Brownfields and RCRA Sites Near 61 Percent of the U.S. Population," October 2021, https://www.epa.gov/cleanups/olem -programs-address-contamination-superfund-brownfields-and -rcra-sites-near-61-percent.

G. P. Jacob, "The Orientation," *Money Power Land Solidarity,* August 22, 2019, https://moneypowerlandsolidarity.libsyn.com/size/5/?search =the+orientation.

I reference "The Orientation," episode 1 of the podcast *Money Power Land Solidarity*. Jacob's podcast covers "issues of land, economic development, politics, race, class and more, all from a working-class left perspective," and has been hugely influential and meaningful to me. I quote and paraphrase some of Jacob's reflections. "North Minneapolis is one of the hearts of the Black community in Minnesota" is quoted. Later, when I write, "It was a place where people experienced poverty and oppression in Minneapolis" I quote Jacob, whose words are, "You could see that people experienced poverty and oppression in Minneapolis."

Terri Hansen, "Kill the Land, Kill the People: There Are 532 Superfund Sites in Indian Country!" *Indian Country Today,* September 13, 2018, https://indiancountrytoday.com/archive/kill-the-land-kill-the-people-there-are-532-superfund-sites-in-indian-country.

Rob Nixon, *Slow Violence and the Environmentalism of the Poor* (Cambridge, MA: Harvard University Press, 2013), 8.

When I write, "I held this place, this maroon-trimmed house, this block of complexity and inequity, in my body in the form of memory, and in the form of industrial particulates that inhabited me epidemiologically, and in the form of grief," I echo Rob Nixon's observation that "if the past of slow violence is never past, so too the post is never fully post: industrial particulates and effluents live on in the environmental elements we inhabit and in our very bodies, which epidemiologically and ecologically are never our simple contemporaries" (8).

Teaching Hospital

Rebecca Altman, "Upriver: A Researcher Traces the Legacy of Plastics," *Orion Magazine,* June 2, 2021, https://orionmagazine.org/article/upriver.

Keisha Brown

Katherine Webb-Hehn, "Dangerous Conditions May Exist in This Area," *SCALAWAG*, June 24, 2019, https://scalawagmagazine.org /2019/06/birmingham-epa-superfund.

Katherine Webb-Hehn, "For Black North Birmingham Residents Fighting Toxic Pollution, Staying Home Isn't Safe," *SCALAWAG*, April 20, 2020, https://scalawagmagazine.org/2020/04/qa-alabama -epa-superfund-covid-19.

Quoted material, as well as some of the paraphrased descriptions of Brown's neighborhood and childhood experiences of asthma, is excerpted from the first article. The second provided more context. With thanks and gratitude to Katherine Webb-Hehn's reporting.

Kathryn Nuernberger, *The Witch of Eye* (Lexington, KY: Sarabande Books, 2021), 75.

Harriman Park, Birmingham, Alabama, © U-Spatial.

From: Keisha Brown

A note on my interview methods: All testimonies began as interviews, using a tape recorder. I then cocreated an essay using the interviewee's own language and rearranging our conversation for flow. I have redacted my questions. Please do not misinterpret these conversations as either persona or a transcript. In all "From" works, multiple versions were discussed and edited, including the final draft. Each interview was a collaboration. Nothing shared here is printed without the explicit consent of the people involved.

All accompanying essays that are narrated from my perspective, in which I am writing about another's life or our time together significantly, were read by those who appear in the works. No representation was singlehanded.

In select instances, names have been changed out of respect and to honor privacy.

I want to thank Keisha Brown for her generosity, and for sharing her story. The last time we spoke on the phone we got on the topic of hope. Keisha shared the following, included here with her permission:

> What gives me hope? I've learned how to be humble. Here, we see people transforming into something that they are not. People deteriorating because they're sick with cancer or sick with something. It's awful to see that. But we're still here. You reached out to me. The truth had to be told. It's like soup—all of us talking. You might bring the corn, someone else might bring the tomatoes. Everybody brings something and we put it together so that we can eat. What I'm saying is, we are the people who are out here living, who are putting everything together for ourselves.

Keisha Brown—in her unwavering generosity—asked me to include the following thanks as well:

> I would like to thank God for the opportunity to tell my story here. I speak not only for my community but for communities all over affected by similar pollution and environmental injustices. I speak up and out against the injustice we face here, daily. All of us. I speak up for the lives of the people among us who suffer the most. I'm glad I was given the opportunity by

Kathryn Savage and Coffee House Press to tell my story in this book.

Some UN Human Rights language and policy is paraphrased and discussed in this testimony. United Nations Human Rights Office of the High Commissioner, "USA: Environmental Racism in 'Cancer Alley' Must End—Experts," March 2, 2021, https://www .ohchr.org/en/press-releases/2021/03/usa-environmental-racism -cancer-alley-must-end-experts?LangID=E&NewsID=26824.

Elizabeth Rush, *Rising: Dispatches from the New American Shore* (Minneapolis: Milkweed Editions, 2018), 256–57.

In Elizabeth Rush's book *Rising*, about rising sea levels and climate change, she asks, "How to tell this story so that it becomes more than elegy alone, both a record of these uncanny times and also a rallying cry?" It is a question I found myself asking too. When I knew that community members' varied experiences living on toxic lands were the truest way to tell this story of place, history, environmental injustice, grief, and health, I drew inspiration from *Rising*, a book that inspired my approach to including community testimony here. I am grateful to Rush and *Rising* for mapping the way from the personal out into the collective.

I am above all else grateful to Keisha, Rebecca, and Gudrun, whose voices are here beside my own. Thank you for the gift of friendship in this work.

Rothstein, Jerome Henry, Artist, and Sponsor Federal Theatre Project, *Don't fear cancer fight it! / JR*. New York, None. [NYC: works progress administration federal art project, between 1936 and 1938]. Photograph. https://www.loc.gov/item/98518521.

Exposure

S. Lochlann Jain, *Malignant: How Cancer Becomes Us* (Oakland: University of California Press, 2013), 184–87.

The title "Exposure" is taken from a subheading in Jain's *Malignant.* Duncan's death is described on page 201.

In the lyric tradition of a work being written "after," this piece is written after Jain's chapter entitled "The Fallout," as it was deeply inspired by their scholarship throughout sections of *Malignant* on legacy and environmental contamination. S. Lochlann Jain is brilliant. I quote and paraphrase Jain throughout "Exposure." I wish to include the original text paraphrased in my essay in full here: "Framing survivorship as a personal accomplishment further separates cancer causation from its manifestations. Cancer becomes a passively occurring hurdle to be surmounted by resolve rather than the direct effect of a violent environment, as incongruous a substitution as a lisp versus a gunshot wound." I have learned so much from them and I am deeply grateful for and indebted to their work.

Suzanne H. Reuben, "President's Cancer Panel 2008–2009 Report on Reducing Environmental Cancer Risk: What We Can Do Now," Department of Health and Human Services April 2010, https://deainfo.nci.nih.gov/advisory/pcp/annualreports/pcp08-09 rpt/pcp_report_08-09_508.pdf.

Writing on paranoia and also on exploring "some of cancer's dissonances," Jain references a 2008–2009 President's Cancer Panel Report on the lack of national policy attention being paid to the public health risks posed by environmental carcinogen exposure (through industrial, military, and agricultural practices). Regarding the need for a comprehensive policy agenda addressing the impact of environmental contaminants on human health, the authors of the report state, "Environmental health, including cancer risk, has been largely excluded from overall national policy on protecting and improving the health of Americans. It is more effective to prevent disease than to treat it, but cancer prevention efforts have focused narrowly on smoking, other lifestyle behaviors, and chemopreventive interventions. Scientific evidence on individual and multiple environmental exposure effects on disease initiation and outcomes, and consequent health system and societal costs, are not being adequately integrated into national policy decisions and strategies for disease prevention, health care access, and health system reform." As Jain observes, though "less than 5 percent of cancer diagnoses can be linked directly to inherited genetic traits," because medical cancer research has long looked to genetics, questioning the environment's role in health can lead one to feel a bit paranoid, and outside the script of cancer.

Cancer Treatment Centers of America, "Stomach Cancer Stages," March 9, 2022, https://www.cancercenter.com/cancer-types/stomach -cancer/stages.

Anne Boyer, *The Undying* (New York: Picador, 2020), 19.

The line "overworked but intoxicated by his own working" quotes Anne Boyer. Her words: "We were overworked, but intoxicated by our own working."

History.com Editors, "Dancer Isadora Duncan Is Killed in Car Accident," September 11, 2019, https://www.history.com/this-day-in -history/dancer-isadora-duncan-is-killed-in-car-accident.

View of a neighborhood home from the Humboldt Yard industrial site © Magali Pijpers.

Toxic Sites

Mel Y. Chen, "Toxic Animacies, Inanimate Affections," *GLQ: A Journal of Lesbian and Gay Studies,* June 1, 2011, 280, https://read.dukeupress.edu/glq/article-abstract/17/2-3/265/34745/Toxic-Animacies-Inanimate-Affections.

> In the summer of 2007, panic about lead paint on Thomas the Tank Engine–brand children's toys, manufactured in China, swept the U.S. media. Fear over the presence of lead paint used militaristic language; the toys were racialized. "Just as the presumed agents of 'terror' have become racialized as Arab and/or Muslim after 9/11, so too has lead itself become recently racialized as Chinese." The subject of harm was often depicted as a middle-class young white boy playing with a train. "For the toy painters," Chen observes, "the conditions of labor needed to be made just visible enough to facilitate the territorial/state/racial assignation of blame, but not enough to generally extend the ring of sympathetic concern around the workers themselves." While toxic load may be useful in understanding environmental harm done to bodies, Chen critiques the by and large Global North theory because it can be weaponized to extend environmental racism in a culture mired in affective language about "invasive threat." As Chen notes, "metaphorical luxuries can have deadly consequences."

Canadian Pacific Shoreham Yard Cedar Service Site, Minneapolis, Minnesota, "Cleanup Progress Update: 15th Issue," December 2019, https://www.cpr.ca/en/community-site/shoreham-repository/Documents/2019%20Final%20Cedar%20Service%20Site%20Annual%20Newsletter%20-%20Approved%20by%20MDA_65845.pdf.

Canadian Pacific and Ashland, Inc., "East Side Shoreham Yard Site Update," July 2019, https://www.cpr.ca/en/community-site /shoreham-repository/Documents/July%202019%20Final%20 East%20Side%20Newsletter%20-%20East%20Side_65924.pdf.

Mailer information and data are summarized from the Canadian Pacific Shoreham Yard facility public document repository website. Information on Shoreham Yards draws from various public documents archived in the repository.

Julia Adeney Thomas, "History and Biology in the Anthropocene: Problems of Scale, Problems of Value." *American Historical Review* 119, no. 5 (2014): 1587–607, http://www.jstor.org/stable/43698892.

Information about the permeable relationship between bodies and places is from Thomas's article, and page 1,601 is quoted and paraphrased. "Our chemical environment *is* us . . . everywhere and with everyone. The old idea that there was a barrier between 'the body' and 'the environment' that could be policed by governments reining in corporations or by individuals making healthy choices no longer pertains as we have come to understand the interpenetrability of bodies and environments."

Safe

The name of the Canadian Pacific representative has been changed.

A Series of Symptoms

Camille T. Dungy, "Is All Writing Environmental Writing?" *Georgia Review,* April 8, 2020, https://thegeorgiareview.com/posts /is-all-writing-environmental-writing.

Dungy's work is enormously instructive to me, and in the space of this essay, I've attempted to meld and draw inspiration from her ecopoetic "concerns of the human world (politics, history, commerce)" with "those of the many life forms with which humans share this planet." Not to do so, echoing Dungy, is "disastrous hubris and folly."

"Shoreham VOC Leak" and "Information on Remedial Activities at Shoreham Yard." I reference the following email exchange, accessed November 3, 2021, https://www.cpr.ca/en/community-site/shoreham -repository/Documents/September%202019%20Release%20at%20 RW07-39-SP%20-%20Notifications%20and%20Followup%20 Reports%20to%20MPCA_East%20Side_65926.pdf.

Miguel Otárola, "Canadian Pacific Takes Rail Yard Off Market, Catching Minneapolis Officials by Surprise," *Star Tribune*, December 2, 2019, https://www.startribune.com/with-rail-yard -expansion-minneapolis-worries-about-uneven-relationship-with -canadian-pacific/565669672/.

Historical and contextual information about Shoreham Yards is paraphrased from this article.

Kathryn Savage, "A Charged Stillness: Tema Stauffer Interviewed by Kathryn Savage," *BOMB,* January 13, 2021, https://bombmag azine.org/articles/a-charged-stillness-tema-stauffer-interviewed.

Greta Gaard, *Critical Ecofeminism* (Washington, DC: Lexington Books, 2019), 143.

Yangho Kim and Jae Woo Kim, "Toxic Encephalopathy," *Safety and Health at Work* 3, no. 4 (December 2012), https://www.ncbi .nlm.nih.gov/pmc/articles/PMC3521923.

The Long Night

Michel Huneault, *The Long Night of Mégantic* (Amsterdam: Schilt, 2016).

The title of this piece is after Michel Huneault's book of photography and transcribed Lac-Mégantic community testimony. In the years after the crash that devastated the town of Lac-Mégantic, Quebec, Huneault spent time with the community impacted by the disaster, bearing witness to their stories. The disaster in Lac-Mégantic evidences the profound consequences of an escalation of seemingly harmless actions. Benign escalation was on my mind as I read about the tragedy that befell Lac-Mégantic and absorbed Huneault's documenting of the community's deeply personal suffering. I am writing this during a week when, in the United States, there have been seven mass shootings in seven days. The stories in Huneault's book are about personal grief in a place transformed after becoming a site of collective suffering. The events in Lac-Mégantic show the myriad ways private grief and public grief and the manifestations of tragedy in individuals, families, and communities both intersect and depart.

Center for Documentary Studies at Duke University, "Post Mégantic" by Michel Huneault, accessed November 20, 2021, https://documentarystudies.duke.edu/exhibits/post-m%C3%A9gantic.

Information about the stores in downtown being opened for eight hours comes from the above source.

Jessica Murphy, "Lac-Megantic: The Runaway Train That Destroyed a Town," BBC.com, January 19, 2018, https://www.bbc.com/news/world-us-canada-42548824.

Christopher Curtis, "Lac-Mégantic: Growing Up after a Tragedy," *Montreal Gazette,* July 6, 2018, https://montrealgazette.com/news /lac-megantic-growing-up-after-a-tragedy.

NCPR News, "NCPR Intern Finds Memory and Grief Just Outside Lac-Megantic Disaster Zone," July 7, 2014, https://www.northcountry publicradio.org/news/story/25348/20140707/ncpr-intern-finds -memory-and-grief-just-outside-lac-megantic-disaster-zone.

Factual and contextual information about Lac-Mégantic, Quebec, and the derailment disaster comes from the preceding sources. Specific data about community mental health consequences is from the *Montreal Gazette.* Further information about how the town collectively grieved can be found via the NCPR source.

Naja Marie Aidt, *When Death Takes Something from You Give It Back* (Minneapolis: Coffee House Press, 2019), 27.

"A night of terror, a cruel night." This is a line after and inspired by Aidt, who wrote: "A night full of terror, a night, a cruel, cruel."

T. J. Demos, *Decolonizing Nature* (London: Sternberg Press, 2016), 101–106.

I was introduced to the installation *Black Shoals Stock Market Planetarium* and the work of Lise Autogena and Joshua Portway through T. J. Demos's book. I quote and paraphrase Demos in my writing on *Black Shoals Stock Market Planetarium.* The paragraph that introduces the night sky installation recalls, quotes, and is deeply informed by his words. In Demos's chapter "The Post-natural Condition," he writes about Autogena and

Portway's planetary ecosystem that is intentionally "devoid of natural life." Demos also writes about the history of marketplace trading on "futures that bet on the outcome of regional temperature fluctuations, rainfall intensity, drought conditions, and hurricanes." He writes, "These mechanisms amounted to financial strategies for corporations to minimize risk to their operations and maximize economic returns, even though this trading is mostly done by speculators without concern for economic or ecological sustainability" (102). Demos presents a thoughtful and nuanced discussion and analysis of artists who are imagining alternative futures to the one trading futures anticipate. Alternative futures that are now "more necessary than ever."

bell hooks, *Belonging: A Culture of Place* (New York: Routledge, 1990), 87–88.

The name of the community garden manager has been changed.

Mary Siisip Geniusz, *Plants Have So Much to Give Us, All We Have to Do Is Ask: Anishinaabe Botanical Teachings* (Minneapolis: University of Minnesota Press, 2015), 190–91.

I am including reference to Anishinaabe botanical teachings published for a general readership to honor the Anishinaabe cultural practices that I continuously learn from in my own relationship with Indigenous lands and in planting. I don't attempt to appropriate Indigenous knowledges but rather to honor the scholars and teachings that shape and inform my thinking. Of the phenomenal Indigenous scholars leading the way in contemporary knowledge production on legacy contamination and environmental actions needed now, I am grateful to Shawn Wilson's *Research Is Ceremony: Indigenous Research Methods;*

Max Liboiron's *Pollution Is Colonialism;* and Elizabeth Hoover's *The River Is in Us: Fighting Toxics in a Mohawk Community.* I have also drawn inspiration from *Represent and Destroy: Rationalizing Violence in the New Racial Capitalism* by Jodi Melamed in my decision to include Anishinaabe botanical teachings in this essay. Melamed draws a useful distinction in her own work, which centers Indigenous scholars. She is not Indigenous and writes "not to lay claim to a field of knowledge or to make pronouncements" that are not hers to make but rather "out of the belief that learning from communally conferred tribal knowledges . . . offers strong opposition to some of the most deadly articulations of power and knowledge at work on the planet" (201–202).

Office of Public Affairs, "Chernobyl Nuclear Power Plant Accident," *Backgrounder,* March 1, 2022, https://www.nrc.gov/reading-rm/doc -collections/fact-sheets/chernobyl-bg.html.

Serge Schmemann. "The Talk of Moscow; Chernobyl Fallout: Apocalyptic Tale and Fear," July 26, 1986, https://www.nytimes .com/1986/07/26/world/the-talk-of-moscow-chernobyl-fallout -apocalyptic-tale-and-fear.html.

Dredge

Wudan Yan, "Superfund, Meet Super Plants," *New York Times,* April 7, 2020, https://www.nytimes.com/2020/04/07/science/superfund -plant-microbiome.html.

Sharon L. Doty, "Using Natural Microbial Symbionts of Trees to Remove Pollutants, Increase Plant Growth, and Produce Biochemicals," University of Washington School of Environmental and

Forest Sciences, November 9, 2013, https://depts.washington.edu /envaplab/documents/PublicWebsite_DotyLabOverview.pdf.

Information about the poplars and the San Francisco Superfund was drawn from the article by Wudan Yan, and further information about poplars and contaminants came from Sharon L. Doty's research.

In my work I paraphrase Yan, who writes, "An hour's drive south of San Francisco, a stand of several hundred poplars grows in a Y-shape—a rather unusual sight wedged between two baseball fields. The trees were planted in 2013 to suck carcinogens out of a 1,500-acre Superfund site contaminated by the U.S. Navy, which disposed of toxic waste generated from developing military aircraft into ponds and landfills."

Illustration of Shoreham Yards © Gudrun Lock.

From: Gudrun Lock

The name of the film referenced is *Call of the Forest: The Forgotten Wisdom of Trees*. It centers the life of Diana Beresford-Kroeger, scientist, conservationist, and author, and was directed by Jeffrey McKay, October 21, 2016.

Thank you, Gudrun, for your friendship and all the good conversations.

Decay Theory

Carnegie Mellon University Libraries, "Five Questions with Harrison Apple," September 15, 2020, https://www.library.cmu.edu/about/news /2020-09/libraries-speakers-series-five-questions-harrison-apple.

The archive lecture was given by Harrison Apple. My lecture notes are paraphrased.

In the Hospital

Lauren Redniss, *Radioactive: Marie & Pierre Curie, a Tale of Love & Fallout* (London: Dey Street Books, 2015), 132.

In the science of decay. . . . In Redniss's stunning book about Marie Curie's life and work I read: "Radioactive elements are unstable. They undergo spontaneous decay. That is, the unstable nucleus emits energetic particles and radiation, thus transforming into an isotope of a different element. This process continues until a stable form is reached. 'Half-life' is the amount of time it takes for half of the nuclei of a given sample to undergo radioactive decay. The primary element is called the 'parent'; the product is referred to as the 'daughter' element." The year he died, my father was sixty-six. I was thirty-three.

Anne Carson, *Glass, Irony, and God* (New York: New Directions Books, 2005), 2.

Halldór Kjartansson and Ari Trausti Guðmundsson, *Living Earth: Outline of the Geology of Iceland* (Reykjavík: Mál og Menning, 2015), 91.

Ronnie Greene, "From Homemaker to Hell-Raiser in Love Canal," Investigating Inequality, Center for Public Integrity, April 16, 2013, https://publicintegrity.org/environment/from-homemaker-to -hell-raiser-in-love-canal.

Information about Love Canal and Lois Gibbs is paraphrased and quoted from this article.

EPA, CERCLA Section 103: Release Notification, accessed April 3, 2022, https://www.epa.gov/epcra/definition-release.

The CERCLA "release" definition is sourced from this webpage.

David Bressan, "How Volcanoes Became a Symbol for Revolution," *Scientific American,* February 19, 2012, https://blogs.scientific american.com/history-of-geology/how-volcanoes-became-a-symbol -for-revolution/.

Information about the social and political history of volcanoes as metaphors is from this source.

Edwidge Danticat, *The Art of Death: Writing the Final Story* (Minneapolis: Graywolf Press, 2017), 152–53.

City of Minneapolis, "Humboldt Industrial Park Redevelopment Plan," December 16, 2005, https://www2.minneapolismn.gov/media /content-assets/www2-documents/government/View-Humboldt -Industrial-Park-Redevelopment-Plan.pdf.

After the Howe chemical fire, sediment was trucked off as waste. . . . Information about the Howe fire and the response taken is sourced from this city report.

"The GAF Shingles Factory with Nancy Przymus," *Money Power Land Solidarity,* September 17, 2019, http://moneypowerlandsolidarity .libsyn.com/the-gaf-shingles-factory-w-nancy-przymus.

Bottineau Neighborhood Association, "A Census Tract-Level Examination of Cancer in Two United States Cities, August 2017, https://bottineauneighborhood.org/wp-content/uploads/2017/08

/Census-Tract-level-Exmination-of-Cancer-and-Asthma-in-two
-U.S-Cities_FINAL.pdf.

"Cancer-Death Maps Reveal Nationwide Patterns," *Minneapolis Star Tribune,* July 20, 1975.

I quoted and paraphrased information from this 1975 U.S. Public Health Study.

Arthur J. Snider, "Air We Breathe to Live May Shorten Our Lives," *Chicago Daily News Service,* December 23, 1960.

The 1960 public health study information is sourced from this article by Snider.

Anne Carson, *Nox* (New York: New Directions, 2010), 3.

Nic Jelinski, University of Minnesota Department of Soil, Water, and Climate, in conversation with the author, February 5, 2019.

The soil facts I've included are taken from my conversations with Nic Jelinski.

"Outside Test of Plant's Emissions Urged," *Minneapolis Star Tribune,* May 12, 1977.

I've quoted and paraphrased information about the 1977 lawsuit from this article.

Don Morrison, "Irate Home Owners Hold Meeting to Protest Railroad Switching Noise," *Minneapolis Morning Tribune,* June 21, 1956.

Quoted and paraphrased information about the 1956 meeting is from Morrison's article.

Rachel Carson, *Silent Spring* (London: Penguin Books, 2015), 170.

Bill Bryson, *Body: A Guide for Occupants* (New York: Doubleday, 2019), 335.

The information I include about fear of earthquakes over cancer is sourced from Bryson's book.

Claudia Rankine, *Don't Let Me Be Lonely: An American Lyric* (Minneapolis: Graywolf Press, 2004), 11.

The information about Gertrude Stein's stomach cancer, as well as Stein's quote, is sourced from Rankine's *Don't Let Me Be Lonely*. In it she writes, "Why do people waste away? The fact that cancer describes a malignant mass of tissue that pulls all nutrients from the body surprises the body first, then the owner of the body, and finally those who look on. Or as Gertrude Stein, who herself died of stomach cancer, points out, 'if everybody did not die the earth would be all covered over and I, I as I, could not have come to be and try as much as I can try not to be I, nevertheless, I would mind that so much, as much as anything, so then why not die, and yet and again not a thing, not a thing to be liking, not a thing.'"

Gertrude Stein, *Wars I Have Seen* (New York: Random House, 1945), 23–24.

Janet Malcolm, "Gertrude Stein's War," *The New Yorker,* May 25, 2003, https://www.newyorker.com/magazine/2003/06/02/gertrude-steins-war.

USGS, "Oklahoma Has Had a Surge of Earthquakes since 2009. Are They Due to Fracking?," accessed June 24, 2021, https://www.usgs.gov/faqs/oklahoma-has-had-a-surge-earthquakes-2009-are-they-due-fracking

> This USGS article is one source I reference for information about earthquakes in states where fracking occurs.

Tip of the Mitt Watershed Council, "Regulations and Exemptions," accessed June 24, 2021, https://www.watershedcouncil.org/hydraulic-fracturing---regulations-and-exemptions.html.

> The Tip of the Mitt Watershed Council source is one I reference for information about hydraulic fracturing under U.S. federal law.

Jon Hamilton, "Town's Effort to Link Fracking and Illness Falls Short," *All Things Considered,* May 16, 2012, https://www.npr.org/2012/05/16/152204584/towns-effort-to-link-fracking-and-illness-falls-short.

> I quote and reference Hamilton's story in my writing about the people of Dish, Texas.

"Ground glass," Wikipedia, accessed November 13, 2021, https://en.wikipedia.org/wiki/Ground_glass.

Kathryn Savage, "On Land," Coffee House Press In the Stacks, August 28, 2019, https://coffeehousepress.org/blogs/chp-in-the-stacks/in-the-stacks-with-kathryn-savage-on-land.

> I incorporate elements of an earlier essay on similar topics, in particular the included references to the ways that chemotherapy interacts with the smell of a person's skin.

Anne Boyer, *The Undying: Pain, Vulnerability, Mortality, Medicine, Art, Time, Dreams, Data, Exhaustion, Cancer, and Care* (New York: Picador, 2020), 49.

Claudius Conrad and James W. Fleshman Jr., eds., *Minimally Invasive Oncologic Surgery, Part 1,* Surgical Oncology Clinics of North America 28, no. 1 (January 2019): xv–xvii, https://www.surgonc.theclinics.com/article/S1055-3207(18)30685-9/pdf.

The quote by Celsus is taken from this source.

On Tenderness

A friend of mine told me this, the story about the rail yard worker and the owl. It's anecdotal knowledge and fair to say that, as such, it can't be proven. Maybe I'm remembering some of the details wrong. As can happen with memory, maybe I've remembered what I *want* to be true—that such small moments of tenderness do take place at industrial sites, between people and animals.

Psychogeography

Andrew S. Mathews, "What Remains," *Arts of Living on a Damaged Planet,* edited by Anna Lowenhaupt Tsing, Heather Anne Swanson, Elaine Gan, and Nils Bubandt (Minneapolis: University of Minnesota Press, 2017), G143–G153.

a man in Monti Pisani, Italy, who walks chestnut forests that lie in ruin due to a long-running nut industry. . . . Information about Mathews and Monti Pisani, as well as quotes, are from *Arts of Living on a Damaged Planet.*

Lauren Elkin, *Flâneuse* (New York: Farrar, Straus and Giroux, 2017), 20–21.

> *"It would be nice, ideal even, if we didn't have to subdivide by gender".* . . . Elkin goes on to write, "but these narratives of walking repeatedly leave out a woman's experience." I found my way to Elkin's thoughtful and expansive scholarship on walking in reading Aminatta Forna's essay "Power Walking" in her collection *The Window Seat: Notes from a Life in Motion* (New York: Grove Press, 2021).

Yi-Fu Tuan, *Space and Place: The Perspective of Experience* (Minneapolis: University of Minnesota Press, 1977), 6.

> Tuan writes, "If we think of space as that which allows movement, then place is pause; each pause in movement makes it possible for location to be transformed into place."

May-lee Chai, *Trespass: Ecotone Essayists Beyond the Boundaries of Place, Identity, and Feminism* (Wilmington, NC: Lookout Books, 2019), xi–xvi.

> Chai writes, "Even without access to literacy, women have sung their stories, woven them into cloth, stitched them into quilts, embroidered them into paj ndau, danced them in ceremonies, chanted them alone and in groups. Women in various cultures have invented their own forms of writing. Some archeologists now believe that the oldest known cave paintings were made by women, based on analysis of handprints on the walls.
>
> "We have trespassed throughout history so that our minds could be free and so that our stories could be told."

Denis Wood, *Rethinking the Power of Maps* (New York: Guilford Press, 2010), 226.

The world as body; the body as world. . . . Denis Wood, on Susanne Slavick's visual and map art work, writes, "Over the years her work has evolved from aerial views of invented topographies, through the manipulation of graticules popularized by 16th- and 17th-century mapmakers (Slavick is especially attracted to the cordiform maps of Mercator and Waldseemüller that enable her to allude to the body, and so to the world as body and the body as world), to work influenced by Gulf War battle plans" (226). I quote and paraphrase Wood in my work.

Bombweed

Rebecca Altman, "On What We Bury," *ISLE: Interdisciplinary Studies in Literature and Environment* 21, no. 1 (Winter 2014): 85–95, https://doi.org/10.1093/isle/isu039.

At the garden, I get to thinking about all that fills dark wombs of the earth. . . . I wish to quote at length from Altman—who has been hugely instrumental to my thinking on burial and seeding, here and elsewhere—who writes,

> I get to thinking how similar the acts of burial and planting are, and what they reflect about our relationship with the Earth and with each other. We open the Earth and place into it seed. We place into it our deceased beloved. We ask the Earth to take what we bury and to give us the solace that comes from cyclical conversion of dormancy and death into transformation or new life. And yet, we also open the Earth and bury what we've wasted, or what we want to hide, and then bury the thought of it. With our landfills, and

our mines backfilled with tailings, our deep injection wells, our caverns of radioactive waste, our faith placed in underground reservoirs of sequestered carbon, we ask the Earth to hold our waste when the Earth isn't static or fixed. It is flux and system and process. There are things that cannot be contained, like glass shards or radioactivity or grief. What I am grappling with here is how we came to believe that certain things we bury could remain outside the cycle of life, or that they would stay where we put them.

"All that fills the dark wombs of the earth" is inspired by Altman's scholarship throughout her essay.

In Crescent Junction, plans are still being made as if stasis should be expected. . . . Altman writes, on the Paradox Basin and the arches in Arches National Park, "These stone monoliths, with their windows and hollowed arches and boulders balanced atop spires, were created by incremental acts of wind and water, and by a restive Earth, forever shifting underneath."

Lindsey Dillon, "Race, Waste, and Space: Brownfield Redevelopment and Environmental Justice at the Hunters Point Shipyard," *Antipode: A Radical Journal of Geography,* October 23, 2014, https://discardstudies.com/wp-content/uploads/2013/04/anti12009_ev3.pdf.

On the persistence of historic erasure in contemporary brownfield redevelopment projects, Dillon writes, "This dominant narrative of an inevitable tide of progress imagines a break with the neighborhood's industrial past, even as hazardous waste endures as a reality for many in the present." Dillon: "For William Jones, who lives in Hunters View and has for decades watched over the old naval base, including the recent, slow process of brownfield remediation, the shipyard is a site of violence and sometimes death. . . . What William described to me was an experience of being left to waste: exposed to the material forms of waste—without sufficient knowledge of or protection from its dangers—and left, more broadly, or neglected, by the state in ways that have manifested in the wasting of human lives through health problems and premature death."

Connective tissue between present and past. . . . Dillon's scholarship explores "connective tissue" between present and past, and waste and space. She writes,

And yet digging up E-2 [a Superfund within the sprawl of brownfields in Bayview-Hunters Point] would also mean another kind of redistribution—that of an even greater amount of contaminated soil from the shipyard to a low-level nuclear waste facility in the desert lands of Tooele County, Utah, near the Skull Valley Goshute reservation. The Skull Valley Goshute tribe already lives with the effects of the Dugway Proving Grounds, the Tooele County Army Depot (the site of the world's largest nerve gas incinerators) and MagCorp—a magnesium production plant which emits chlorine gas (Jeffries 2007). Even without the removal/displacement of E-2, thousands of truckloads of soil from the shipyard have, in the past few years, been deposited in Tooele County. In short, brownfield redevelopment—now a generalized urban strategy—represents a new challenge for the environmental justice movement, in terms of thinking through what justice might mean in such circumstances where the toxic by-products of twentieth century industrialization must ultimately be confronted and lived with by humans and other creatures at some time and place. Here, the concept of waste formations attempts to bring emerging theoretical approaches on waste together with ideas of environmental justice in a way that recognizes these new socio-ecological problems of the twenty-first century.

Her scholarship explores ways of thinking *less* in terms of a return to "pristine nature" but instead, encourages the imagining of "a new, hybrid form of post-industrial nature emerging in and through the ruins of an industrial past."

Clarence Hightower, "Quindaro, Kansas, A Symbol of American Urban Decline," *Minnesota Spokesman Recorder,* August 31, 2016, https://spokesman-recorder.com/2016/08/31/quindaro-kansas-symbol -american-urban-decline.

Cut off from the rest of Kansas City by the path of the Missouri Pacific Railroad, the Missouri River, and interstate highways. . . . I quote and paraphrase Hightower, who writes,

The Quindaro neighborhood is one of the most industrially polluted places in America, with the local coal-fired power plant directly causing a multitude of illnesses and even deaths each year. This is without a doubt a cruel and disheartening fate for such a historically significant and once proud place. . . . America's communities require dialogue, empathy and reconciliation. . . . So, where do we begin?"

Quindaro's geographic location and its placing on the historic register quotes and summarizes Hightower.

Anne Boyer, *A Handbook of Disappointed Fate* (Brooklyn: Ugly Duckling Presse, 2018), 32–41.

Some strangers, the same sad world. . . . this is a Boyer quote (31).

Kansas City–based writer Anne Boyer observes. . . . Boyer writes, "There is a problem for a poet who lives in a city like this. There is, along with the brutality, the aesthetic allure of ruins and the long Western poetic tradition of admiring them. Like many "ruined" Midwestern cities, there is the problem of "art" in Kansas City, and of artists and gentrifiers and lifestyle. It is a problem that exists precisely because of the aesthetic allure of a city like this, and its cheap space and cheap lawlessness: these vacancies created by white supremacy and capital" (39).

Shadow Mountain

Kelly Bostian, "It Used to House a Zinc Smelter. Now the Collinsville Superfund Site Houses Rescued Honeybees," *Tulsa World,* July 31, 2019, https://tulsaworld.com/news/local/it-used-to-house -a-zinc-smelter-now-the-collinsville-superfund-site-houses-rescued -honeybees/article_2f8ea6d8-d0e9-501a-810c-3407f0a51ec8.html.

EPA, "EPA Celebrates 20 Years of Superfund Redevelopment; Recognizes Restored Site in Collinsville, Okla., for Reuse as Honeybee Habitat," July 31, 2019, https://www.epa.gov/newsreleases/epa -celebrates-20-years-superfund-redevelopment-recognizes-restored -site-collinsville.

Information about the Collinsville smelter comes from the two sources above.

Patricia Shannon, "This Pretty Orchid Looks Just Like a Bumble Bee (And It Helps Attract Them, Too!)," *Southern Living,* accessed November 15, 2021, https://www.southernliving.com/garden/flowers /bee-orchid.

Nicholas Shapiro, "Attuning to the Chemosphere: Domestic Formaldehyde, Bodily Reasoning, and the Chemical Sublime," *Cultural Anthropology* 30, no. 3 (2015): 368–93, https://journal .culanth.org/index.php/ca/article/view/ca30.3.02.

I quote and paraphrase Shapiro's scholarship throughout this essay. Shapiro observes, "Bodies uncover invisible toxins with their wounding" (384). His work on bodily attunement to environmental and domestic toxicants positions itself as "the beginning of a confrontation, not its resolution" (381). Shapiro writes, "If bodily reasoning is the dynamic process through which knowledge of individual spaces of chronic exposure is somatically attained, the chemical sublime is the accrual of bodily reasoning to the point of articulating the patterned practices and infrastructures that distribute pockets of exposure across space. It is the traversing of a threshold of chemical awareness whereby the *irritations* of one's immediate environment become *agitations* to apprehend and attenuate the effects of vast toxic infrastructures" (380).

Éireann Lorsung, *The Century* (Minneapolis: Milkweed Editions, 2020), 6.

Anna Lowenhaupt Tsing, Heather Anne Swanson, Elaine Gan, and Nils Bubandt, eds., "Introduction: Haunted Landscapes of the Anthropocene," *Arts of Living on a Damaged Planet* (Minneapolis: University of Minnesota Press, 2017), M4.

Property Relations

Bertolt Brecht, "Writing the Truth: Five Difficulties," translated by Richard Winston, in *Civil Liberties and the Arts: Selections from Twice a Year, 1938–48,* edited by William Wasserstrom (Syracuse, NY: Syracuse University Press, 1964), 295.

The title "Property Relations" and the Brecht quote are both taken from this source.

"Saint Germaine Cousin," Wikipedia, accessed November 14, 2021, https://en.wikipedia.org/wiki/Germaine_Cousin.

Marguerite Mills, "Exodus: Living and Leaving the North Side," May 22, 2020, https://storymaps.arcgis.com/stories/695d1dcd10194 addb331eebc5a21de73.

The phrase "performances of white violence" quotes Marguerite Mills's cartography scholarship on private property, spatially racialized discriminatory financing policy, and cross-cultural trauma in U.S. cities. Mills writes, "The areas of the city, now concentrated with minority residents through racially restrictive covenants, were deemed 'hazardous' for bank investment. And it became nearly impossible to secure a loan to purchase property in the areas of the city where people of color now lived." These processes "cemented a myth" of "segregated white space as desirable, safe, and inherently valuable."

Mills's work explores individual, collective, and city-scale trauma. When I spend time with her work, I am reminded that to exist within a place is more than being there; it is also to hold community scars. Much of her work centers on the contemporary and historic violence of private property ownership in Minneapolis. Her maps and essays explore places as being like bodies in that both are locations of "trauma and resilience." Mills writes, "Ourselves and our bodies hold intergenerational and family traumas, and place holds cross-cultural traumas. It holds oppressor and oppressed. Place bodies hold our community scars and hidden histories. Place bodies hold networks of care, roadmaps of revolution. . . . Place holds the muscle memory of healing." Quotes included in this paragraph reference Mills's "Place Keeps the Score: An Atlas of Collective Trauma and Radical Healing in Minneapolis," accessed November 15, 2021, https://mills278.wixsite.com/mcmills/copy-2-of-project-09.

Timothy Otte, "notes toward an incomplete understanding of cartography," manuscript in-progress, 19.

> I am grateful to Timothy Otte's manuscript in-progress, "Landscape Quartet: notes toward an incomplete understanding of cartography," the work to which I owe the line "Our lives are shaped by empire / our lives shape the land." Quoted with his permission. Thank you for your kindness, insights, and all the good talks, Timothy.

Mary Siisip Geniusz, *Plants Have So Much to Give Us, All We Have to Do Is Ask: Anishinaabe Botanical Teachings* (Minneapolis, University of Minnesota Press, 2015), 184–91; 216–23.

> *Mullein thrives on newly turned soil, so it is one of the first plants to regrow after a woodland has been clear-cut.* . . . Information about roadside mullein, ancient England, and mullein stalks as "witch's candles" is paraphrased from 184–85. For more on jewelweed and animal interactions, see the examples on 222–23.

Kathryn Savage, "Witch Trials, Symbiotic Mutualism, and the Poetry of Fury and Yearning: A Conversation with Kathryn Nuernberger," *World Literature Today,* June 10, 2020, https://www.worldliteraturetoday.org/blog/interviews/witch-trials-symbiotic-mutualism-and-poetry-fury-and-yearning-conversation-kathryn.

> *I recall what my friend Kate said about what cocktail ants do.* . . . I quote and paraphrase a conversation between us in this essay. With thanks to Kate, for your friendship and endless brilliance, and for letting me quote you here.

Sianne Ngai, *Ugly Feelings* (Cambridge, MA: Harvard University Press, 2007).

"Between the white paint and Germaine, I feel disgust" honors Sianne Ngai's seminal affect theory scholarship. In her *Ugly Feelings,* she critiques ecofeminism that hinges on hunches, on poetic-paranoia. She advocates for, rather than a poetry of ecological paranoia, the embrace of a lyricism of disgust. "In its intense and unambivalent negativity, disgust thus seems to represent an outer limit or threshold of what I have called ugly feelings, preparing us for more instrumental or politically efficacious emotions." I strive to push my own ecological paranoia to a point that is more "politically efficacious" (354).

Wasteland

Anagha Srikanth, "The Carbon Footprint of Cancer Care," *Changing America,* May 18, 2020, https://thehill.com/changing-america /sustainability/climate-change/498342-the-carbon-footprint-of -cancer-care.

> *U.S.-hospital cancer care requires considerable amounts of energy; the pharmaceutical industry is 50 percent more carbon intensive than the automotive industry.* . . . The information I include about the energy involved in cancer care and its related pharmaceutical industry is drawn from this article.

Urns Northwest, "Are Human Ashes Bad for the Environment?," February 16, 2021, https://urnsnw.com/articles/are-human-ashes -bad-for-the-environment/.

> *The by-products of burning a life include fine soot, carbon monoxide, sulfur dioxide. Mercury from dental filling.* . . . This information is paraphrased from the above article.

Rebecca Altman, "On What We Bury," *ISLE: Interdisciplinary Studies in Literature and Environment* 21, no. 1 (Winter 2014): 85–95, https://doi.org/10.1093/isle/isu039.

My "We also bury seeds, I realized, we plant our dead and our desires for more life in the same earth" isn't a direct quote, but the idea is indebted to Rebecca Altman's scholarship on inter-generational body-burden, burial, birth, and planting seeds from her essay "On What We Bury."

Roads to Take

Rebecca Altman, "Who Sings from the Resins?," *Orion Magazine,* August 2021, https://orionmagazine.org/article/who-sings-from-the -resins.

There are hardly any markers in Hawk's Nest to memorialize the disaster. . . . I paraphrase Altman's scholarship on Raymond Thompson Jr.'s photography and archival work. Altman writes, "Thompson honors 'the history of those left behind.' Deliberately, he celebrates their lives, their American experi-ence, as he put it. All to correct 'historical amnesia,' to counter the institutionalized erasure, gaps in the archival record that feed into partial and damaging histories parceled into boxes, when in fact the histories interconnect: energy systems with metals with chemicals with plastics with racism with war-making with nationalism."

Rebecca Altman, "Upriver," *Orion Magazine,* Summer 2021, June 2, 2021, https://orionmagazine.org/article/upriver/.

"These are roads to take when you think of your country". . . . my opening paragraph paraphrases Altman's introduction to

Rukeyser's work. In my descriptions of the disaster at Hawk's Nest, I have relied on contextual and descriptive language from Altman's essay. Please see her excellent essay "Upriver" to learn more about Hawk's Nest and its intersections with the complex legacy of plastics.

My refrain of Rukeyser's *roads to take* is also after Altman, who also refrains this line in her essay.

Muriel Rukeyser, *The Book of the Dead* (Morgantown: West Virginia University Press, 2018), 61, 96.

Adelina Lancianese, "Before Black Lung, The Hawks Nest Tunnel Disaster Killed Hundreds," NPR, January 20, 2019, https://www.npr.org/2019/01/20/685821214/before-black-lung-the-hawks-nest-tunnel-disaster-killed-hundreds.

In Hawk's Nest, the Union Carbide and Carbon Corporation is at work constructing a three-mile tunnel in 1930. . . . I paraphrase Lancianese's reporting.

Bryan Nelson, "10 Places Ruined by Human-Caused Catastrophes," Treehugger, September 22, 2021, https://www.treehugger.com/places-ruined-by-man-made-catastrophes-4869131.

Quapaw Nation, "Environmental," accessed November 18, 2021, https://www.quapawtribe.com/563/Environmental.

Dates and details about the history of the Quapaw Nation are from this source.

LEAD Agency (Local Environmental Action Demanded), https://www.leadagency.org.

In Picher, contamination from lead and zinc pit mines extending hundreds of feet under homes. . . . Years of extensive research inform my writing on the Tar Creek Superfund. Included contextual information is also provided by the Quapaw Nation and the LEAD Agency.

Alex Anderson, "Tar Creek Remade: Taking on 120 Years of Environmental Injustice at an Oklahoma Superfund Site," June 15, 2021, https://www.gsd.harvard.edu/2021/06/tar-creek-remade-taking-on-120-years-of-environmental-injustice-at-an-oklahoma-superfund-site.

At the turn of the twentieth century, found to be mineral-rich, this swath of prairie was force-leased by the U.S. government and sold to private mining companies. . . . I found my way to Niall Kirkwood's work on landscape architecture, remediation, and imagining alternative futures in Tar Creek through Rebecca Jim. Some of the historical context I include is taken from the above essay that also details Kirkwood's teaching landscape architecture students about community-centered approaches to collective envisioning of slow transformations in brownfield remediation work and "a healing landscape." Anderson writes, "At the outset of 'Tar Creek Remade,' Kirkwood cautioned the students to consider that in their designs, what matters is not "the 'stamp' or 'signature' of the author" but "ethical and cultural attitudes to land, landscape and the natural world" and a genuine concern for the people who work to repair the land and who live on that land."

Raymond Thompson Jr. and Rob Simmons, "Appalachian Ghosts— Story Behind the Art," December 2, 2019, https://vimeo.com/376951187.

Thompson reflects, in the film on his photographic work, "History's been written by the winners in society. They decide what is collected and kept to tell new histories. So I'm interested in the histories of the people who were left behind." Thompson describes his photographic work as a celebration and not a memorial.

Raymond Thompson Jr., "Artist Statement," accessed November 19, 2021, http://www.raymondthompsonjr.com/artist-statement.

Thompson's artist statement on his photographic series inform my descriptions of his work.

Floodwaters

"Skaitook Lake, Oklahoma, USA," LakeLubbers.com, accessed April 4, 2022, https://lakelubbers.com/lake/skiatook-lake-oklahoma-usa.

I credit this source for contextual information about Skiatook, Sand Springs, Sapulpa, and Tulsa using lakes as water supply as well as the U.S. Army Corps of Engineers relationship to the pit lake.

Oklahoma Historical Society, "Osage County," *The Encyclopedia of Oklahoma History and Culture*, https://www.okhistory.org/publications/enc/entry.php?entry=OS004.

Chris DiMaria, "8 Year Old Battles with E. coli Exposure after Lake Swim," 2News Oklahoma, June 27, 2019, https://www.kjrh.com/news/local-news/8-year-old-battles-e-coli-exposure-after-lake-swim.

Contextual information about the child with kidney disease was originally reported on by Chris DiMaria of CBS Tulsa local news.

The Zone

Andrei Tarkovsky, *Stalker* (Mosfilm, 1979; Criterion Collection, 2017, new restoration), DVD.

Mel Y. Chen, "Toxic Animacies, Inanimate Affections," *GLQ: A Journal of Lesbian and Gay Studies,* June 1, 2011, 280, https://read.dukeupress.edu/glq/article-abstract/17/2-3/265/34745/Toxic-Animacies-Inanimate-Affections.

Rob Nixon, *Slow Violence and the Environmentalism of the Poor* (Cambridge, MA: Harvard University Press, 2013), 6.

Andrei Tarkovsky, *Sculpting in Time: Reflections on the Cinema* (Austin: University of Texas Press, 2017), 38.

T. J. Demos, *Decolonizing Nature* (London: Sternberg Press, 2016), 45–47.

My phrasing *European and American pollution-driven environmental art and theorizing that emerged during the 1960s and '70s* . . . owes acknowledgment to Demos's *Decolonizing Nature.* My inclusion of Bateson's work (and quote) is also from Demos's comprehensive and historic work. For more on the intersections and representations of ecological art from the 1960s on, please see Demos. He has been very influential to my own thinking on Tarkovsky and his contemporaries.

Gregory Bateson, "Up against the Environment or Ourselves?," *Radical Software* 1, no. 5 (Spring 1972): 33 (emphasis in original).

Mark Le Fanu, "*Stalker*: Meaning and Making," Criterion, July 18, 2017, https://www.criterion.com/current/posts/4739-stalker-meaning -and-making.

My phrase "The film was shot in Estonia near the capital of Tallinn. . . ." paraphrases and quotes Le Fanu, who went on to write, "[*Stalker* was] shot in the vicinity of physically dangerous materials, without much thought given to protecting the crew or the actors. . . . There are people close to Tarkovsky's legacy who swear that the cancer that killed him, and possibly others, had its origins in the terrible months of *Stalker*'s multiple shootings."

Tar Creek and chat piles in Picher, Oklahoma, © U-Spatial.

Coronal CT reconstruction and PET scan, from T. Vag et al., "PET Imaging of Chemokine Receptor CXCR4 in Patients with Primary and Recurrent Breast Carcinoma," *EJNMMI Research* 8, no. 90 (2018): fig. 1a–b, is licensed under CC BY 1.0.

Chat Piles

Stephanie Buck, "The Oklahoma Town That Produced Most of WWI's Bullets Is Now a Poison Graveyard," *Timeline*, August 9, 2017, https://timeline.com/picher-oklahoma-lead-toxic-186e5595232b.

My descriptions of chat and pollution were informed by Buck's essay.

Lia Purpura, *On Looking: Essays* (Louisville, KY: Sarabande Books, 2006), 6.

My "How easily my body opens. . . ." quotes Purpura's "How easily the body opens."

Downstream

Max Liboiron, *Pollution is Colonialism* (Durham, NC: Duke University Press, 2021), 24–25; 34.

Liz Blood and Joseph Rushmore, *O'River* (Tulsa, OK: Walls Divide Press, 2019), 7, 20, 24.

> *Time laps the banks* references Blood, who writes, "Time laps your banks."

Moira Villiard, Illuminate the Lock: *Madweyaashkaa: Waves Can Be Heard,* installation 2021, accessed December 6, 2021, https://parkconnection.org/illuminate; and Suenary Philavanh, "Resilient: Searching for Connections through Waves," February 17, 2021, http://northern.lights.mn/2021/02/resilient-searching-for-connections-through-waves.

Quapaw Tribe, https://www.quapawtribe.com/401/Tribal-Name, accessed November 21, 2021.

Photo of Superfund Cleanup didactic © Magali Pijpers.

Felicity Barringer, "Despite Cleanup at Mine, Dust and Fear Linger," *New York Times,* April 12, 2004, https://www.nytimes.com/2004/04/12/us/despite-cleanup-at-mine-dust-and-fear-linger.html.

> As of 2017, the Tar Creek Superfund site remains one of the largest and most challenging Superfund sites to remediate in the country. In a 2004 *New York Times* piece, Felicity Barringer, on Tar Creek, writes: "Like a patient riddled with overlapping infections, Tar Creek has exhibited almost every symptom of a modern wasteland. . . . The site is a stark reminder of the limits

of the federal government's ability to clean up the messes of the industrial age."

Steve Ward, "As Almost Generational Trust Litigation Ends, the Quapaw Finally Get a Settlement," *American Indian Law,* November 20, 2019, https://www.cwlaw.com/newsletters-84.

In 2019, after years of litigation, the Quapaw Nation reached an agreement with the United States in a multimillion-dollar settlement to "obtain a measure of justice for serious federal mismanagement of its reservation lands, accounts, and other Indian trust assets." From the Nation's press release: "Under a settlement with the United States, the Nation and its members are due to receive almost $200 million through a combination of immediate payments and appropriations to be requested from Congress. . . . This settlement represents symbolic justice for the wrongs done to the Quapaw people through the federal government's mismanagement of our lands and other assets."

From: Rebecca Jim

I am grateful to Rebecca Jim for leading the way, and for all the good conversations. Thank you.

Tar Creek

OK Energy Today, "Flooding Might Have Increased Dangers of Tar Creek Superfund Site," June 6, 2019, http://www.okenergytoday .com/2019/06/flooding-might-have-increased-dangers-of-tar-creek -superfund-site.

Tar Creek and chat pile © Magali Pijpers.

Watershed

Rebecca Jim, "Local Environmental Action Demanded," *The LEADer,* Spring 2021.

> "Tar Creek must be addressed as a matter of environmental justice," Rebecca Jim writes in LEAD's spring 2021 newsletter. She advocates that Congress reauthorize the Superfund Fee under CERCLA. Over twenty years ago, this fee, also known as the "polluter-pays" tax, expired. "Reauthorizing the Superfund polluter-pays provision will provide cleanup money so citizens do not have to pay for cleanup." For added context, Lacy M. Johnson, writing on the polluter-pays provision, observes, "For the last twenty years, there has been no fund funding the Superfund." See *The Reckonings: Essays* by Lacy M. Johnson (New York: Scribner, 2018), 305. Further action is needed now. The action should include the new EPA Region 6 administrator ordering, Jim writes, "a new Remedial Investigation and Human Health Risk Assessment that is more protective of human health and the environment. The health of communities around Tar Creek can no longer be ignored and set aside as an accepted casualty of historic mining." She points out, "Indigenous people from nine tribes make up more than 20 percent of the population in the county, with many individuals having ancestry in multiples tribes." In her discussion of rising coasts and trees, Jim is referencing Elizabeth Rush's book *Rising* (Minneapolis: Milkweed Editions, 2018).

I paraphrase Jim's letter and also some of our other conversations in this essay.

Julietta Singh, *The Breaks* (Minneapolis: Coffee House Press, 2021), 3–4.

Bound (i.5), 2019, Exhibition: "Beyond Measure," photo by Phil Maisel, courtesy of Tali Weinberg.

What Is Birthed?

Tali Weinberg, *Bound,* 2017–2019, https://www.taliweinberg.com /inextricably-bound.

> The didactic quoted appeared in an August 29, 2021 email announcing Tali's solo show *Water Ways* that took place at Praxis in Cleveland, Ohio, September 2021. I attended *Bound* in Tulsa. As the didactic was iterative, and emerged out of Tali's earlier work, she has granted permission for descriptive melding in this essay.

> Thank you, Liz Blood, for your friendship and your willingness to be quoted.

Donna Haraway, *Staying with the Trouble: Making Kin in the Chthulucene* (Durham, NC: Duke University Press, 2016), 35.

Sandra Steingraber, *Living Downstream: An Ecologist's Personal Investigation of Cancer and the Environment* (Boston, MA: Da Capo Press), 2.

> Sandra Steingraber's book on ecology and cancer has been very influential to my own thinking throughout this essay. When I write "Water flows within a diffuse net of permeable vessels like the movement of fluid inside bodies," I am referencing her writing on the similar movement patterns of water and blood. Both flow "within a diffuse net of permeable vessels. So too in Illinois, a capillary bed of creeks, streams, forks, and tributaries lies over the land." When I write "I live both up- and downstream," I am paying tribute to her important work.

Terry Tempest Williams, *When Women Were Birds: Fifty-Four Variations on Voice* (New York: Picador, 2012), 104.

The movements of blood and milk. . . . I am echoing Terry Tempest Williams's writing on the body. "Milk and blood live together" is a quote from Williams's *When Women Were Birds.*

Lacy M. Johnson, "What Slime Knows," *Orion Magazine,* Autumn 2021, https://orionmagazine.org/article/what-slime-knows/.

I think about how legacy ecological violence and other legacies of white supremacist thought and action thrive on imagining a world of separations and hierarchies. . . . When I write this, I am thinking about Lacy M. Johnson's scholarship on historic racism in taxonomy and the violence of the Anglo-white imaginary in ecological discourse, and also—seemingly unrelated, but she ties the two topics together brilliantly—the awesomeness of slime molds. Johnson writes,

> Taxonomy has evolved in the centuries since Haeckel and Linnaeus, but much of their thinking still remains. Even if science no longer views humans as divided into different and unequal species, we continue to refer to 'race' as if it were a natural, biological category rather than a social one created in service of white supremacy. The myth that humans are superior to all other species—that we are complex and intelligent in a way that matters, while the intelligence and complexity of other species does not—also exists in service to white supremacy, conferring on far too many people an imagined right of total dominion over one another and the natural world.

Rebecca Altman, "On What We Bury," *ISLE: Interdisciplinary Studies in Literature and Environment* 21, no. 1 (Winter 2014): 85–95, https://doi.org/10.1093/isle/isu039.

Inheritor of my ancestors' trash and misdeeds. . . . Rebecca Altman's children play at a hilly playground near her house that used to be the Reed Brook municipal landfill. The hill, she writes, is "a mound of our forebears' trash." As is evident throughout this work, Altman's scholarship is very influential to my own thinking. In writing on body burden and the impact of toxins on future generations, I frequently recall Altman.

How?

Nick Flynn, "Killdeer," Poets.org, January 4, 2018, https://poets.org /poem/killdeer.

These are the lines I quote as they appear in "Killdeer": "whatever / inside us that we think needs / protection, the whatever that is / small & hasn't yet found its / way. And later: it thinks it could live / on air, on words, forever almost."

With deep thanks to Nick Flynn for allowing me to include these lines in my work.

Keep Out

"Keep Out," 2019 © Victoria Hannan.

Shotgun Fungi

Mary Oliver, "Spring," *House of Light* (Boston, MA: Beacon Press, 1992), 6.

Linda Treeful, Cynthia Ash, Rebecca Brown, Chad Behrendt, and Crystal Floyd, "Common Fungi in Yards and Gardens," University of Minnesota Extension (2018), https://extension.umn .edu/lawn-care/common-fungi.

Anna Lowenhaupt Tsing, *The Mushroom at the End of the World: On the Possibility of Life in Capitalist Ruins* (Princeton, NJ: Princeton University Press, 2021), viii, 1, 137–39.

> *It's like they've got everted stomachs. . . .* Tsing writes, "Fungi have extracellular digestion. They excrete digestive acids outside their bodies to break down their food into nutrients. It's as if they had everted stomachs, digesting food outside instead of inside their bodies. Nutrients are then absorbed into their cells, allowing the fungal body to grow—but also other species' bodies."

> *But sometimes harmony breaks down. . . .* Tsing writes, "Mutual benefits do not lead to perfect harmony. Sometimes the fungus parasitizes the root in one phase of its life cycle. Or, if the plant has lots of nutrients, it may reject the fungus. A mycorrhizal fungus without a plant collaborator will die. But many ectomycorrhizas are not limited to one collaboration; the fungus forms a network across plants. In a forest, fungi connect not just trees of the same species, but often many species."

> I paraphrase and reference Tsing's work in my own.

Acknowledgments

Thank you Keisha Brown, Rebecca Jim, and Gudrun Lock, for sharing your words about healing bodies and places with me, and filling these pages with your commitment to community and ecology. Thank you for reading every version of your testimony, for your candor and strength. I can never properly repay you for agreeing to be part of *Groundglass*. When Maggie Nelson writes, "The heart, too, is porous," I think about our conversations over the years, full of grief, but also humor and joy. Please know that your friendship has been my healing.

Thank you to the following magazines and journals for publishing portions of this work, sometimes in different forms: *Ecotone Magazine* ("Mullein" and "Safe"), *BOMB Magazine*, *Menagerie Magazine* ("Shadow Mountain" and "The Soo Line Dump"), the *Virginia Quarterly Review* ("At the Tar Creek Superfund Site"), and *World Literature Today* ("The Long Night"). Thank you to the generous and incisive editors Sophia Stid, Anna Lena Phillips Bell, Raluca Albu, Steve Woodward, Allison Wright, Heidi Siegrist, and Daniel Simon.

Thank you, Coffee House Press, and special thanks to my kind, brilliant, and exacting editor Lizzie Davis. Thank you Anitra Budd, Daley Farr, Chris Fischbach, Erika Stevens, Marit Swanson, Carla Valadez, and the whole team. Thank you Annemarie Eayrs, Laurie Herrmann, Kellie Hultgren, and Stacey Parshall Jensen. Thank you Samantha Shea.

For sharing your time, insights, and expertise, and talking with me about everything from your work and advocacy to your experiences of family and place, I am ever grateful to Tom Bierlein, Christine Brown, Mike Curran, Kirsten Delegard, Kristi Eaton,

Dr. Rachel R. Hardeman, Nic Jelinski, Ryan Mattke, Marguerite Mills, Abby Moore, Roxxanne O'Brien, Christopher Pexa, Kate Probst, Nancy Przymus, Todd Stewart, William Toscano, Jake Virden, Loren Kasey Waters, Dr. Elizabeth Wattenberg, Tali Weinberg, and Nathan Young. Thank you to the countless scientists, scholars, and writers whose work shaped my thinking and writing, in particular Kazim Ali, Rebecca Altman, Anne Boyer, Mary Siisip Geniusz, bell hooks, Max Liboiron, and Sandra Steingraber. Thank you to the publishers, authors, and artists who extended permission to have your work quoted and included here.

Thank you to my students and colleagues at Augsburg University, Hamline University, MCAD, the University of Minnesota, and St. Cloud State University. Thank you to my teachers and classmates at the Bennington Writing Seminars, the University of Minnesota, and The New School. For providing support and community, thank you Bread Loaf Writers' Conference, Grand Marais Art Colony, the Loft Literary Center, Minnesota Prison Writing Workshop, Minnesota State Arts Board, and Tulsa Artist Fellowship. Thank you, mother in words, Rebecca Chace, for believing in me. Paul Yoon, thank you for being an extraordinary writer and mentor. Thank you, Kathryn Nuernberger, for seeing what I couldn't see and loving this book into being. I am forever grateful to all my teachers and mentors. You light the way with your words.

My deep appreciation goes out to Victoria Blanco, Liz Blood, Rebecca Brill, Eleanor Garran, Ray Gonzalez, Victoria Hannan, Jessica Harvey, Douglas Kearney, Daniel Kossow, Mariela Lemus, M. L. Martin, Katie Moulton, Timothy Otte, Susan Pagani, Roseanne Pereira, Erin Kate Ryan, Nathan R. Stenberg, and Allison Wyss—for reading, talking, and sharing your wisdom with me so that this book might grow.

Beloved friends, thank you for being part of my life. For your influence and encouragement as I shaped these pages, thank you Julie Alpert, Jennifer Bowen, Charlie Baxter, Yanna R. Demkiewicz, Jenny Dodgson, Sara Fowler, Kate Gunther, Su Hwang, Ginny and Peter Janelle, Michael Kleber-Diggs, Keith Lesmeister, Rhett McNeil, Ben Moren, Rajesh Parameswaran, Angela Pelster, Drew Peterson, Bao Phi, Peter Price, Ruth Pszwaro, Mary Austin Speaker, Tema Stauffer, Patricia Straub, Paul Solum, Katherine Rochester, Max Ross, Damon Tabor, Josh Theroux, Christina and Kawai Strong Washburn, Sherrie Fernandez-Williams, and Diane Wilson. Thank you, Kate Boyle. For your generosity as I rounded the final lap, thank you Rebecca Heidenberg and Gregory Smith. Taylor Dees, Molly Fuller, Corey Lawson, Lindsay Mound, and Magali Pijpers—I would be lost without your love; you are family. Thank you, Dad, for being beside me and for your love. Thank you, Mom, for your nurture and bravery. Thank you, Nana and Andrew, for your endless care and effusiveness. Thank you, Jim, for your writer's faith; and Beth, for being lovely. Thank you, beloved Holmquists and Hershleders. Thank you, Jason, and the Savages. Thank you, Solimans, for welcoming me. Moheb, I love you. Henry, oh, how I love you.

Coffee House Press began as a small letterpress operation in 1972 and has grown into an internationally renowned nonprofit publisher of literary fiction, essay, poetry, and other work that doesn't fit neatly into genre categories.

Coffee House is both a publisher and an arts organization. Through our *Books in Action* program and publications, we've become interdisciplinary collaborators and incubators for new work and audience experiences. Our vision for the future is one where a publisher is a catalyst and connector.

LITERATURE
is not the same thing as
PUBLISHING

Funder Acknowledgments

Coffee House Press is an internationally renowned independent book publisher and arts nonprofit based in Minneapolis, MN; through its literary publications and Books in Action program, Coffee House acts as a catalyst and connector—between authors and readers, ideas and resources, creativity and community, inspiration and action.

Coffee House Press books are made possible through the generous support of grants and donations from corporations, state and federal grant programs, family foundations, and the many individuals who believe in the transformational power of literature. This activity is made possible by the voters of Minnesota through a Minnesota State Arts Board Operating Support grant, thanks to the legislative appropriation from the Arts and Cultural Heritage Fund. Coffee House also receives major operating support from the Amazon Literary Partnership, Jerome Foundation, McKnight Foundation, Target Foundation, and the National Endowment for the Arts (NEA). To find out more about how NEA grants impact individuals and communities, visit www.arts.gov.

Coffee House Press receives additional support from Bookmobile; Dorsey & Whitney LLP; Elmer L. & Eleanor J. Andersen Foundation; Fredrikson & Byron, P.A.; the Matching Grant Program Fund of the Minneapolis Foundation; Mr. Pancks' Fund in memory of Graham Kimpton; the Schwab Charitable Fund; and the U.S. Bank Foundation.

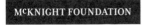

The Publisher's Circle of Coffee House Press

Publisher's Circle members make significant contributions to Coffee House Press's annual giving campaign. Understanding that a strong financial base is necessary for the press to meet the challenges and opportunities that arise each year, this group plays a crucial part in the success of Coffee House's mission.

Recent Publisher's Circle members include many anonymous donors, Patricia A. Beithon, Anitra Budd, Andrew Brantingham, Dave & Kelli Cloutier, Mary Ebert & Paul Stembler, Jocelyn Hale & Glenn Miller, the Rehael Fund-Roger Hale/Nor Hall of the Minneapolis Foundation, Randy Hartten & Ron Lotz, Dylan Hicks & Nina Hale, William Hardacker, Kenneth & Susan Kahn, Stephen & Isabel Keating, the Kenneth Koch Literary Estate, Cinda Kornblum, Jennifer Kwon Dobbs & Stefan Liess, the Lambert Family Foundation, the Lenfestey Family Foundation, Sarah Lutman & Rob Rudolph, the Carol & Aaron Mack Charitable Fund of the Minneapolis Foundation, Gillian McCain, Malcolm S. McDermid & Katie Windle, Mary & Malcolm McDermid, Daniel N. Smith III & Maureen Millea Smith, Peter Nelson & Jennifer Swenson, Enrique & Jennifer Olivarez, Alan Polsky, Robin Preble, Jeffrey Sugerman & Sarah Schultz, Nan G. Swid, Grant Wood, and Margaret Wurtele.

For more information about the Publisher's Circle and other ways to support Coffee House Press books, authors, and activities, please visit www.coffeehousepress.org/pages/donate or contact us at info@coffeehousepress.org.

These words were written in Minneapolis and Tulsa, on the traditional, ancestral, and contemporary lands of Indigenous people, the homelands of the Dakota and Ojibwe people and of the Osage, Cherokee, and Muscogee people.

A percentage of the sale of this book will support work being done by the Local Environmental Action Demanded (LEAD) Agency of Miami, Oklahoma, and the Greater-Birmingham Alliance to Stop Pollution (GASP), Birmingham, Alabama. Both organizations take action to counter environmental hazards and stand up for healthy water, air, and environmental justice through education, advocacy, and collaboration.

Learn more at:
https://www.leadagency.org
https://gaspgroup.org

Kathryn Savage's writing has appeared in *American Short Fiction,*
Ecotone Magazine, the *Virginia Quarterly Review, BOMB,* and the
anthology *Rewilding: Poems for the Environment.* Recipient of the
Academy of American Poets James Wright Prize, she has received
support from fellowships and residencies including the Bread
Loaf Writers' Conference, Minnesota State Arts Board, Ucross
Foundation, and Tulsa Artist Fellowship. She lives with her family
in Minneapolis and teaches creative writing at the Minneapolis
College of Art and Design.

Groundglass was designed by Bookmobile Design & Digital Publisher Services. Text is set in Adobe Garamond Pro.